Early Experience
and the Life Path

By the same authors

A.D.B. Clarke and A.M. Clarke (1966, 1969, 1975) *Recent Advances in the Study of Subnormality*. London: N.A.M.H.

A.D.B. Clarke and A.M. Clarke (eds) (1973) *Mental Retardation and Behavioural Research*. London: Churchill Livingstone.

A.M. Clarke and A.D.B. Clarke (eds) (1958, 1965, 1974) *Mental Deficiency: The Changing Outlook*. 4th edition with J.M. Berg (1985). London: Methuen and Glencoe, Ill.: Free Press.

A.M. Clarke and A.D.B. Clarke (eds) (1976) *Early Experience: Myth and Evidence*. London: Open Books and New York: Free Press.

of related interest

Vulnerability and Resilience in Human Development
A Festschrift for Ann and Alan Clarke
Edited by Barbara Tizard and Ved Varma
ISBN 1 85302 877 0

Six Theories of Child Development
Revised Formulations and Current Issues
Edited by Ross Vasta
ISBN 1 85302 137 7

Child Development for Child Care and Protection Workers
Brigid Daniel, Sally Wassel and Robbie Gilligan
ISBN 1 85302 633 6

Early Experience and the Life Path

Ann M. Clarke and Alan D.B. Clarke

Jessica Kingsley Publishers
London and Philadelphia

This edition first published in the United Kingdom in 2000 by
Jessica Kingsley Publishers Ltd,
116 Pentonville Road,
London N1 9JB,
England
and
325 Chestnut Street,
Philadelphia, PA 19106, USA.

www.jkp.com

Copyright © 2000 Ann M. Clarke and Alan D.B. Clarke

ISBN 1-85302-858-4

Library of Congress Cataloging in Publication Data
A CIP catalogue record for this book is available from the Library of Congress

British Library Cataloguing in Publication Data
A CIP catalogue record for this book is available from the British Library

Printed and Bound in Great Britain by
Athenaeum Press, Gateshead, Tyne and Wear

To Thomas and Emma, their parents and Peter

The doctrines which best repay critical examination are those which for the longest time have remained unquestioned

(A.N. Whitehouse, quoted by Stevenson 1957)

Contents

Preface

Two studies, published in 1954, initiated the thesis which we develop in this book. The first, by Hilda Lewis, documented the improved status of children legally removed from their parents. The second, our own findings, charted the cognitive (and later social) recovery in mildly learning disabled or backward adolescents and young adults, drawn from situations of cruelty or neglect. These publications appeared just three years after Bowlby's influential and deeply pessimistic monograph (see Chapters One and Five).

At first puzzled by our findings, we combed the literature for earlier straws in the wind, publishing some of these in 1953. Several areas seemed to us to be relevant. First, the reports in the early 1930s on the outcome of some of the first longitudinal studies. Second, the results of the classic Harvard Growth Study (Dearborn and Rothney 1941). Third, the often poorly controlled work of the Iowa Group (e.g. Skeels and Dye 1939) which nevertheless emphasized the malleability of development. Fourth, a review by Orlansky (1949) which suggested that particular child-rearing practices (e.g. type of toilet training) possessed no adult personality correlates. Last, a single, well-conducted prospective study of backward and retarded children which showed, on average, an improved status in adulthood (Charles 1953). These straws in the wind were not insubstantial, and were soon to be backed up by studies of the outcome for previously malnourished children who exhibited physical recovery after improved nutrition, a rebound effect very similar to our psychological findings.

By 1958/59 we began to believe that our findings would generalize very widely. Our publishers urged us to write a book on the theme that there could be substantial recovery from the effects of early deprivation provided better circumstances allowed this. We began to write, but confronted with a dearth of empirical evidence, we put this material 'on hold'. Sixteen years later we felt that research findings had become overwhelmingly in favour of our thesis, so in 1976 we edited and were major contributors to *Early Experience: Myth and Evidence*. This book included offerings by eminent researchers such as Urie Bronfen-brenner, Alfred Kadushin, Jerome Kagan, Michael Rutter and Barbara Tizard.

Following the book's publication we continued to monitor the field in a succession of review articles (e.g. 1984, 1992). By 1996 we concluded that there was overwhelming evidence for the long-term complexity of human development, suggesting 'a degree of unpredictability for the individual, a principle of developmental uncertainty' (p.48).

In a sense, the present sequel to the 1976 book should be un-necessary, other than as a historical review. But it has to be more than this, for a belief in the special, disproportionate, long-term effects of early experience is deeply embedded in a very common view of development. Such a belief obscures the rich interplay, throughout life, of personal and social influences and can have unfortunate implications (see Chapter Seven).

Many researchers have contributed to this field, and we are grateful to all of them. The names of four, however, stand out for their major contributions: Professors Stella Chess and Alexander Thomas, Jerome Kagan and Sir Michael Rutter. To these our personal debt is very considerable. We are also grateful to Dr Janet Carr who drew our attention to important work we had missed, and to Professor Barbara Tizard who offered constructive suggestions for Chapters Six and Seven.

We are also indebted to our publisher, Jessica Kingsley, her team and especially our editor, Amy Lankester-Owen, for their enthusiastic and helpful support.

Finally, we must express our great appreciation for Maria Harrison's immense help in producing this book. Her good-humoured de-ciphering of sometimes difficult script in the first draft, and her identification of occasional repetitiousness, have made its completion a pleasure rather than a pain.

A.M.C. and A.D.B.C.   September 1999

CHAPTER ONE

Prologue

Signpost: *The origin and development of the thesis*

A number of philosophers throughout the centuries have speculated about human development – or what nowadays we would call lifespan development. Thus Plato (428–348 BC) wrote: 'And the first step ... is always what matters most, particularly when we are dealing with the young and tender. This is the time when they are taking shape and when any impression we choose to make leaves a permanent mark.'

Or again, Quintilian (c. AD 35–100): 'We are by nature most tenacious of what we have imbibed in our infant years, as the flavour, with which you scent vessels when new, remains in them ...'

Much more recently, John Locke (1632–1704) wrote: 'The little or almost insensible impressions on our tender infancies have very important and lasting consequences ...'

Writing in 1796, Samuel Smith suggested:

> Were man able to trace every effort to its cause, he would probably find that the virtue or the vice of the individual, the happiness or misery of the family, the glory or the infamy of a nation had their sources in the cradle ... (quoted by Kagan 1979, p.13)

The final philosopher to be quoted is James Mill (1816):

> As soon as the infant, or rather the embryo, begins to feel, the character begins to be formed; and that the habits which are then contracted, are the most pervading and operative of all.

These statements, dating from ancient times, suggest a degree of predetermination in human development based on the child's earliest experiences. This is one version of what came to be known as the constancy model; that is, when particular characteristics are formed in the child, no further changes relative to age peers, are likely. By the beginning of the twentieth century a further predeterministic view began to be aired: Spearman (1904) stated that intellectual function appears to become fully developed in children by about their ninth year, and possibly even much earlier. 'From this moment, there normally occurs no further changes even into extreme old age.' It is of interest that this view could not have been based on empirical work, since by 1904 no proper follow-up studies had been undertaken. Only one man, Alfred Binet, stood out against this view; writing in 1911, the year of his death, he argued:

> Some recent philosophers appear to have given their moral support to the deplorable verdict that the intelligence of the individual is a fixed quantity, a quantity which cannot be augmented. We must protest and act against this brutal pessimism. We shall endeavour to show that it has no foundation whatsoever ... (quoted posthumously in Binet 1920)

Nevertheless, Spearman's view led directly to the assumption that the IQ is constant, formally proposed a few years later by Stern.

Similar predeterministic theses emerged in the field of emotional development. Thus Freud (1910) wrote:

> On the other hand we must assume, or we may convince ourselves through psychological observation on others, that the very impressions which we have forgotten have nevertheless left the deepest traces in our psychic life, and acted as determinants for our whole future development.

In a posthumous publication (1949) he added:

> It seems that neuroses are only acquired during early childhood (up to the age of six), even though their symptoms may not make their appearance until much later ... analytic experience has convinced us of the complete truth of the common assertion that the child is psychologically father of the man and that the events of his first years are of paramount importance for his whole subsequent life ...

A further example from the early part of this century came from J.B. Watson (1928), the founder of Behaviourism. He was a strange bedfellow with Freud:

> But once a child's character has been spoiled by bad handling, which can be done in a few days, who can say that the damage is ever repaired? ... some day the importance of the first two years of infancy will be fully realized ... Children's fears are home grown just like their loves and temper outbursts. The parents do the emotional planting and the cultivating. At three years of age the child's whole emotional life plan has been laid down, his emotional disposition set. At that age the parents have already determined for him whether he is to grow into a happy person, wholesome and good-natured, whether he is to be a whining, complaining neurotic, and anger driven, vindictive, over-bearing slave driver, or one whose every move in life is definitely controlled by fear.

However, unlike Spearman, he was honest enough to indicate that these views were not based on empirical work, but represented informed speculation.

Post-War Research

We come now to the immensely influential work of John Bowlby (1951) who had prepared a monograph for the World Health Organisation. He summarized his views as follows:

> Among the most significant developments in psychiatry during the past quarter of a century has been the steady growth of evidence that the quality of the parental care which a child receives in his earliest years is of vital importance for his future mental health ... it is this complex, rich, and rewarding relationship with the mother in the early years, varied in countless ways by relations with the father and with siblings, that child psychiatrists and many others now believe to underline the development of character and of mental health ... the evidence is now such that it leaves no room for doubt regarding the general proposition – that the prolonged deprivation of the young child of maternal care may have grave and far-reaching effects in his character and so on the whole of his future life.

He added that good mothering was almost useless if delayed beyond two and a half years.

The whole emphasis in this work was on mother–child separation, and the monograph in which were reviewed a wide variety of mainly poorly controlled studies depended, in particular, on three important ones. First, Bowlby (1946) examined the histories of 44 juvenile thieves, finding that in a substantial minority there had been prolonged maternal–child separation. Second, a number of studies by Goldfarb were reported. The 1943 publication, for example, recorded very different outcomes for 15 children adopted early, and another 15 institutionally reared from six months to three and a half years before adoption. When followed up between 10 and 14 years, those adopted later were markedly inferior on all measures to the early adopted children. It seems likely that selective factors favoured early versus later adoption, and therefore compounded the effects of institutional rearing (see discussion in Chapter Six). Finally, a series of papers by Spitz (1945, 1946a, 1946b) seemed to support Bowlby's thesis. The studies took place in an unidentified institution in an unnamed country and showed horrifying pictures of developmental deceleration, high mortality from a measles epidemic and progressive dehumanization. As many subsequently have indicated, these children lacked not only maternal care but lacked care. As we shall see, Bowlby was later to modify his views (e.g. 1956, 1988).

Our own studies and their sequel

In 1951 (the same year as the publication of Bowlby's monograph) we were asked to reopen a psychology department founded and then abandoned by several psychologists in a very low-cost institution. This hospital contained some 1400 persons compulsorily detained under legal order, some three-quarters of whom were mildly retarded or, in some cases, merely backward. These were mainly adolescents or young adults who either had caused social problems or were regarded as at risk of perpetrating maladjusted or criminal behaviour in the community, and were regarded as a eugenic threat.

Two apparently unrelated streams of research followed, both of which gave results in the teeth of received wisdom. The more important, relating to this book, was the accidental discovery that some of our mildly retarded individuals in adolescence and early adulthood showed marked increments in IQ and social adjustment. A number of hypotheses were examined; these included the possibility that younger members would have made greater increments, that test practice might be responsible, that to be a recent admission to the hospital might result in underestimation because of emotional upset and hence a later spurious increment, and that those with lower IQs might show greater improvements. None of these appeared especially important; however, it was established that a record of earlier severe, prolonged social adversity predicted later improvement. The rating of severe adversity depended on the presence in the individual case history of at least 2 of 12 specific criteria indicating an early record of cruelty and neglect that had led to official action to remove the child from the parents (Clarke and Clarke 1954). Conversely, less severe adversity or its absence in the background was associated with a poorer prognosis for IQ increments, social adjustment and discharge from care. After a pilot study, a 'clean' series of studies were initiated, in which assessment was carried out independently by a colleague without knowledge of social history or earlier test scores, and another independent researcher without knowledge of the individual or test scores rated childhood history for the degree of adversity (severe or less severe).

Altogether we undertook four studies, although our results were recorded in a number of articles in addition to the primary sources. The first (Clarke and Clarke 1954) investigated the frequency of IQ changes over two and a quarter years and their relationship to earlier severe adversity. We began to wonder whether these findings would generalize to other deprived children rescued from adversity, and were at once rewarded by the results of Hilda Lewis's (1954) study. Using only a two-year follow-up of children taken temporarily into an assessment centre, having been removed legally from their parents, she found major improvements in their psychiatric status. We were able to discuss our own research personally with Bowlby, who noted the intellectual increments as very encouraging.

We were soon greatly cheered by the increasing evidence of physical catch-up following illness or malnutrition which seemed to us to parallel our own findings of psychological resilience. Later such processes were termed the 'self-righting tendency', which promotes individual recovery to the greatest extent allowed by new and better circumstances (Waddington 1966).

The second, third and fourth studies were all reported by Clarke, Clarke and Reiman (1958). The second study employed a four-and-a-half-year test–retest time interval, confirming larger changes in relation to the longer time interval. The third increased the test–retest interval to six years. Some 78 per cent of the severely deprived group showed increments of 15 or more IQ points, compared with some 25 per cent of the less deprived group. The fourth study showed that changes were *not* related to differences within the institutional programmes, but represented a fading of the effects of earlier adversity – a self-righting tendency. Finally, we studied a control group of consecutive new admissions, reassessed after three months, enabling an estimate to be made of the greatest possible effects of statistical regression toward the mean and test practice. On average, these accounted for, at the most, only a quarter of the six-year increments.

The late or delayed development occurring in the most deprived mildly retarded persons seemed to represent one of several factors accounting for the marked decrease in administrative prevalence from adolescence onward, which is common in epidemiological research. For example, Richardson (1985, p.374) reported some results from the Aberdeen study in which five birth-year cohorts were followed from ages 5 to 22. After school-leaving age (15–16 years) the prevalence of those receiving mental retardation services decreased by more than half, a drop accounted for by formerly designated mild cases, there being no change in the number of more severely retarded.

Subsequently, our four studies were replicated several times elsewhere. For example, Svendsen (1982, 1983) in Sweden followed to adulthood a sample of educable mentally retarded and slow-learning children. Estimates of early family and personal problems showed that IQ changes were associated with the greater number of problems and with post-school education. Increments in the 'problems' group averaged 18 IQ points, compared with five points in the group with one or no problems and without further education. Somewhat similar findings are recorded by Roswell Harris (1958), Brown (1972) and Duyme, Dumaret and Tomkiewicz (1999).

This, then, was a problem that found the researchers rather than *vice versa*. It challenged the notion of a necessary developmental constancy, a view that has dominated developmental theory for most of the twentieth century (Brim and Kagan 1980; Clarke and Clarke 1984). It also challenged the idea that the events of the first few years have a crucially formative influence. The early experiences of our 'adverse' young people could scarcely have been more damaging. Indeed, their compulsory incarceration provided testimony to their earlier disturbed behaviour and significantly sub-average intellectual functioning. But these effects tended to fade. As noted, improvements were much less common in those with backgrounds of less severe or no adversity. It seemed probable that these findings might generalize (e.g. Clarke and Clarke 1959, 1960).

An early and wide-ranging review by Stevenson (1957) passed almost unnoticed. He examined recent data on the plasticity of development at different ages, noting that there is no predictable relationship between specific child rearing practices and later personality. He added that severe stresses can have as marked effects in adults as in children, and sometimes these are greater in the former. Important personality changes can occur after childhood, including the disappearance of some disorders. Moreover, a lack of new experiences in childhood may give the appearance of a more fixed personality pattern than in fact it is potentially. He concluded that the case for a greater plasticity of infant and childhood personality compared with adulthood remained open. His review threw doubt on the assumption that early experience was of paramount importance in the formation of adult personality. It was a matter of regret that we did not find this article until 20 years later!

During the 1960s, most of the published evidence appeared to go against our hypothesis and to support the existence of psychosocial critical periods very early in life. The work of the ethologists was very influential; and Harlow (1963), Levine (1960) and Scott (1963, 1968) all published experimental results showing the long-term adverse effects of early deprivation in animals. While accepting the usefulness of animal studies at neural levels, we were very sceptical about the extrapolation of some of the results to social and educational problems in disadvantaged children.

So far as Harlow's work on the later maladjustment of formerly isolated monkeys was concerned, we took this very seriously indeed, but lamented that an equal amount of ingenuity had not been spent constructing experiments that might reverse the damage. We argued that if, following isolation experiences, these monkeys had not been transferred to an improved, remedial situation, then a self-perpetuating cycle of maladjusted behaviour might be expected. There was no evidence that any such attempt had been made. Much later this problem was addressed by Novak and Harlow (1975) and Suomi and Harlow (1972), whose results were in keeping with our own hypothesis.

There was also the problem of the many human studies that showed merely a correlation between early environmental circumstances and later behavioural status, without demonstrating a clear environmental change in between, strictly speaking the only valid test of the crucial effect of the early period. Finally, to our great surprise, Skeels (1966) entitled his important monograph *Adult Status of Children with Contrasting Early Life Histories: A Follow-Up Study* (our emphasis), again following the *Zeitgeist* of the 1960s. This research seemed clearly to be a study of children who had been shifted around a good deal during the 'critical years' (Skeels and Dye 1939) and then fortunately had been adopted (albeit late) and remained in stable, accepting homes. The outcome in adult life was thus almost certainly as much a product of their happy adoptive status as of their early experiences (see Clarke 1982; Clarke, Clarke and Berg 1985 pp.9,10). Furthermore, one child who had been left in the institution, but given exceptional help, was found to be the 'star' individual in the contrast group.

By 1975 we believed that there was sufficient evidence to produce a book that suggested that early experiences, good or bad, did not in themselves set for the child an invariant life path. Contributions were included from such scholars as Urie Bronfenbrenner, Jerome Kagan, Michael Rutter and Barbara Tizard. It was stressed that our conclusions should not be interpreted literally as a counterbalance, which might be an equal and opposite extreme, but rather as an attempt to achieve a balanced view. With one or two discordant voices, reviewers seemed to feel that in *Early Experience: Myth and Evidence* (Clarke and Clarke 1976) a valid case had been made for a greater degree of potential open-endedness in human development than had until then been accepted.

Summarizing the main arguments, we indicated that there is no known adversity from which at least some children had not recovered if moved to something better and that the whole of the life path is important, including the early years. These are, of course, foundational in nature, leading in most cases to confirmatory influences, as age increases. Three additional points were also made. First, increasing age probably imposes constraints on potential responsiveness to environmental influences. This may be intrinsic to the aging process or may result from habit, forced or chosen life paths, and social pressures. For want of a better analogy we called this a 'wedge' model, with the thick end representing early potential responsiveness to change, tailing off to the thin end much later in life.

Second, one way in which early experience effects may be perpetuated, usually indirectly, is when one good or unfortunate thing leads to another and a chain of good or bad events then follows. For example, a maladjusted child in care may not be considered for fostering or adoption and, therefore, will remain in a less than satisfactory institution. The maladjustment may remain, and continue to manifest itself on further examination, with consequent failure to intervene strongly.

Third, it seemed possible that early adversity, overcome by improved circumstances, might nevertheless leave the individual potentially more vulnerable to later stress. Experiences that affect the individual's behaviour in more than a transitory way must involve learning, broadly defined. Stress might reawaken earlier maladjusted behaviour in the same way that unused skills are more easily relearned after the passage of time.

Traditionally, researchers often sought powerful single main factors leading to single main effects; however, many variables may be involved in an outcome. These are not necessarily solely additive; some studies have shown potential multiplicative effects of two, three or four variables (Rutter *et al.* 1975a, 1975b). Identifying six risk factors in childhood, Rutter *et al.* showed that the occurrence of one yielded no greater risk than was evident in control children. Two resulted in a fourfold increase, and four factors produced a tenfold increase in emotional and conduct disorders.

Genetic factors (e.g. Rutter *et al.* 1999a), constitutional factors and micro-, meso- and macroenvironmental trajectories represent headlines for the complex processes involved in human development. Bronfenbrenner (1977) and Bronfenbrenner and Crouter (1983) have elegantly described the various components of environments as their differing levels interact with the individual (e.g. home, peer group, school, economic conditions and culture). He also described these processes as lifelong. One should also add transactions; there is empirical evidence that, to some extent, individuals create or choose their own environments, receiving reinforcing or modifying feedback (e.g. Bell 1968; Scarr and McCartney 1983; Thomas, Chess and Birch 1968). Finally, chance encounters or events sometimes potently alter the course of development.

Because of its fortuitous nature, the role of chance has largely been ignored, Bandura (1982) being a notable exception. For example, mature students entering higher education frequently cite a chance event such as redundancy as having played a significant part in what, for them, is a major life change. Or again, a serious accident may suddenly have imposed limitations on development. The point is made in a poetic metaphor by Milosz (1988): '… sometimes one pebble is enough to determine the direction in which the avalanche of a man's destiny is to roll' (p.51). People also differ in their capacity to use for their own benefit, or for avoidance of the effects of chance events or encounters.

We now revert to the important, and perhaps less obvious, concept of transactions. The work of Chess and Thomas anticipated much of what was later to be recognized. From 1956 onwards, when they initiated the classic New York Longitudinal Study (see Chapter Three), they were well aware of the importance in development of the child's temperamental qualities and the two-way parent–child interaction. As child psychiatrists they were of course especially interested in the orig-ins and development of behaviour disorders (e.g. Chess and Thomas 1984; Thomas and Chess 1980), and the 'goodness of fit' between the individual's temperament and the parents' expectations and demands. To paraphrase the authors' definition, 'goodness of fit' results when environmental expectancies are congruent with the child's own capacities, characteristics and style of behaving, leading to optimal development. Conversely, poorness of fit arises from discrepancies between the individual's capacities and the opportunities and demands of the environment. Such situations, if ongoing, carry a risk of maladaptive functioning (Chess and Thomas 1999).

Although Chess and Thomas have written extensively about transactions, the development of this concept is usually accredited to Sameroff and Chandler (1975), in a very important chapter. They concluded that both individuals and their environments are potentially plastic, with the former as active participants in their own development.

In these four major influences, it is the first, genetic factors, which have been revealed much more clearly in the last couple of decades. As Rutter et al. (1999a) put it in a notable review, 'through twin and adoption studies [it is clear that] genetic influences are important across the whole range of human behaviour and not just in relation to disorders ...' (p.8). As we have indicated, what is also apparent is that genetics (the genotype) does not precisely determine the outcome (the phenotype). For most characteristics there is often a wide range of response to environment. For example, stature is strongly influenced by heredity, but if you, the reader, had been brought up in a famine area, you would be far shorter than your present height.

Even an armchair analysis of these overly simple headlines would suggest enormous complexity in human development, and that the probable non-linearity of each variable, let alone in combination, would indicate some degree of unpredictability in the long term of *individual* (as opposed to group average) life paths. Of course, these influences do tend to co-vary. For example, the naturally intelligent child is likely to be reared in caring, stimulating circumstances, and with a 'good' temperament (if lucky), to receive transactional feedback and more chance opportunities than his/her less favoured peer. Furthermore, Plomin (1994) has pointed out that environmental effects on behavioural development largely involve non-shared environmental processes which make children in the same family different from one another.

It is easy to forget that development must always occur within its historical context, especially at times of dramatic change. For example, the Great Depression produced sometimes immense changes for families (Elder 1974); so did World War II, and in China, the Cultural Revolution. In many cases, the life chances and opportunities for individuals were altered for ever. As Elder (1998) puts it, the Great Depression suggested 'a world out of control', yet 'families often worked out successful adaptations within available options and constraints'; others did not. Elder notes the 'cumulation of advantages and disadvantages' and stresses the timing of transitions for the strength of such effects. Thus, in the follow-up of the Terman study of highly able children, the older cohort of men entered the Great Depression and war years at 'an untimely point' of their lives and tended to follow a path of lifelong disadvantage in comparison with the younger group. However, the emphasis of Elder's many studies is on the many successful adaptations in the teeth of historical disasters, not gained without personal cost in having to cope with life stresses (Elder 1998).

Summary

We have outlined the origins of our thesis that the effects of early experiences, important at the time, will only be prolonged if similar experiences follow. We have stressed the complexities of development and the need, therefore, to study the role of genetic, psychosocial, transactional, chance and historical variables and their interactions in the life courses of individuals.

CHAPTER TWO

Some Research Problems ... and Solutions

Signpost: *Longitudinal methods, their advantages and difficulties*

In this chapter it is the writers' aim to draw attention to four basic problems in longitudinal research. These are (1) the probable difference in outcome in retrospective versus prospective research on the same problem; (2) the potentially distorting influence of sample loss on follow-up results; (3) the limits to generalization and the possibility of sample specificity; (4) environmental continuities versus change, as well as the crucial role of the latter in evaluating the effects or otherwise of early experience.

Longitudinal methods

1. Retrospective

The *retrospective* (follow-back) approach can be relatively rapid, and therefore cheaper than the prospective (follow-forward) method. Starting as it does with a clearly delineated group, retrospective studies will often have available earlier records, sometimes supplemented by interviews, giving a picture of the individual's or group's past life path. Since these are often concerned with unusual samples (e.g. criminals, psychiatric patients), and since to attain the label of 'unusual', some lapse of time is to be expected, continuities in personal histories are common, and often strong. For example, in such individuals one bad period can be followed by, and lead to, further bad periods *ad infinitum*, hence the likelihood of continuity. One problem with the retrospective method is that, while continuities may be apparent, there is no way of knowing how many had similar experiences yet failed to develop in the way characteristic of the identified group.

2. Prospective

The *prospective* method is lengthy, expensive and often deals with a more heterogeneous population than does the retrospective. Outcome is likely to be much more varied than those in retrospective samples who almost by definition form relatively homogeneous groups. Sample loss can be a major problem, possibly biasing the overall results since this is usually a selective attrition. For example, if one follows up a socially deprived population and, many years after first identification, a minority is untraceable, it is likely that the 'lost' members will to some extent have escaped the consequences of their early life. This means that the remaining 'captive', non-mobile members are likely to have done less well than the 'lost'. Overall results will thus give a gloomier picture than would be justified for the original, total group. On the other hand, if a pre-school programme loses its less promising members, the average for the remainder will be higher. Empirical examples have been provided in a summary article by Wolke *et al.* (1995). It is very important to document drop-outs, write these authors, in following up pre-term children;

> mothers with low educational attainments and those with infants with serious developmental delay or disability are most likely to drop out of surveillance programmes ... parents who have not come to terms with their child's developmental deficits may tend to avoid situations where these difficulties are highlighted ... It is worrying that more poorly educated mothers and their very pre-term infants who would benefit most from early intervention are most difficult to keep in follow-up studies. (p.443)

Without tracing such drop-outs who do badly, a better overall picture obtains for the rest and this may be wrongly generalized to *all* very pre-term infants.

Most researchers try to cope with the problem of sample loss by checking that early assessments for those lost were on average no different from those retained. This is like saying that everyone is equal at the start of a race, and will therefore remain equal at the finish. The lesson here is to avoid sample loss by every means and this depends on resources, both human and financial.

3. The problem of measurement

There is also the *problem of measurement*. Whether in physics, biology or psychology, all measurement involves error, even though in some sciences the error may be infinitesimal or very small. Because of daily personal fluctuations which may be completely insignificant in the long term, measurement errors can be significant in the behavioural sciences. Supposing an individual under-functions (for example, for emotional reasons, or from fatigue in some baseline assessment) yet later functions normally, a spurious increment may be noted. So, more than two (and preferably many more) measures across time are necessary to detect trends. These personal fluctuations tend to cancel each other out in repeated measurements. And then there is the problem of deciding at the outset of a prospective longitudinal study which measures are to be used later, remembering that cost may be important.

To recapitulate, it is to be expected that retrospective and prospective studies will not yield exactly the same answers to the same research question. The starting point for a retrospective study is often a homogeneous population traced backwards over somewhat similar life paths. For a prospective study, divergent life paths over time are common when followed onwards from baseline, especially if the latter is assessed very early in life when development is rapid and fluctuant.

Often researchers have been concerned with single factors with predeterministic potential. There is always the possibility that each may reflect wider influences than the factor itself. For example, a record of separation between parent and child, especially if often repeated, may occur in the context of some disastrous situation, and a correlation between the particular factor, in this case separation, may if taken on its own, mask a constellation of other diversities.

4. The range of data presented

It may be important in presenting data to include the ranges of scores as well as means and standard deviations; for a fine example see O'Connor *et al.* (1999a), who, best of all, include a scattergram thus enabling readers, if they so wish, to carry out further analyses using all the basic information.

5. Independent assessment

Whenever possible, ratings or other measures should be assessed by independent researchers *blind* to the hypothesis and to other assessments. It is well known that expectancies can both affect data collection or its interpretation.

6. Clinic samples and limits to generalization

Much research in developmental psychiatry and some in developmental psychology has arisen, as earlier noted (p.23), in the study of clinic samples. But not all disordered individuals find their way to clinics. Are those who do not less affected than those who do? Or is it sometimes a matter of chance whether referral or self-referral takes place? It seems a reasonable guess that, by and large, the more seriously disordered persons will be found in the retrospective clinic samples, and if so, generalization to non-clinic individuals may be overly pessimistic. This likelihood is certainly supported in studies of the outcome for those who in childhood had suffered sexual abuse. A pessimistic picture is presented in a notable review of what must have been mainly clinic samples (Stevenson 1999) compared with a less gloomy situation for a substantial number of children reflected in a study of a random sample of the general population reporting in adulthood a history of sexual abuse and its effects or non-effects (Mullen *et al.* 1993, 1994).

Case studies and research on groups

Valuable lessons may be derived from following up individual severely deprived children after rescue. Here again there may be selective reportage of those who benefited versus those who made unsuccessful adaptations. The findings, however, would be replicated, although in a minor key, in investigations of the outcome for less severely deprived children moved to a better situation. If dramatic recovery are the findings in the former case, less dramatic findings, but in the same direction, are to be expected in the latter, less damaged children. So there is a probable congruence between the two forms of study (see Chapters Four and Five).

Environmental continuities versus change

In attempting to identify the role of early experience in later development, there are a number of additional problems which need to be outlined. Under ordinary circumstances children experience some continuities of care. For example, 'good' care in early life tends to be followed by the same qualities later; so, too, with 'bad' care, 'average' care or 'inconsistent' care. Hence any early effects are likely to be reinforced subsequently. This being so, one would expect, if anything, enhanced correlations between early and later (even adult) characteristics. The next chapter will offer information on the results of such research. A note of caution must, however, be issued. Early characteristics are usually very different from later; for example, intelligence as measured at age two has little obviously in common with intelligence at adolescence. While the former may possess seeds of the latter, many intellectual processes are undeveloped or unformed at the early age. Moreover, genetic programmes do not necessarily follow straight paths (see Wilson 1985), so in essence it may be very difficult to interpret links which exist. And if such links are not very strong, this would be expected from the foregoing. Perhaps broader early and later assessments might show more interpretable information.

A second approach will be less equivocal. One needs to study before and after effects on development when some sharp change in the child's circumstances occurs. Here are two examples: suppose that the child has 'good' early experiences until age three. These are followed by prolonged adversity. Do the former provide protection against the effects of the latter? Now suppose that a child has 'bad' early experiences followed by a strong, positive intervention. Does the latter overcome the effects of the former? This approach provides the toughest test of the permanence, or otherwise, of the effects of early experience. In practice, there is a great deal more information on the changes from 'adverse' to 'good' than *vice versa*, and Chapters Four onwards will sample these researches.

Summary

Retrospective and prospective studies of children under ordinary circumstances will identify the strength of links between early and later characteristics. Since retrospective investigations tend to relate to homogeneous 'unusual' groups, these links will be stronger than is found in prospective data where wider ranges of outcome are usually involved. For many individuals, behavioural characteristics tend to alter differentially under natural conditions, in spite of social and educational pressures, than tend to keep children on a self-fulfilling prophetic path. Such qualities in turn may affect and reflect the social context for good or ill. Additionally, in addressing the longitudinal method, some attention was paid to generalizing from clinic samples to wider populations. This is part of the common problem of recognizing the possibility of sample specificity in research findings. Finally, sample loss in prospective studies is a major hazard in long-term research.

CHAPTER THREE

Development under 'Natural' Circumstances

Signpost: *Normally there are both continuities and changes in long-term development, but early characteristics are only poorly correlated with their adult equivalents*

Towards the end of the 1920s and the early 1930s, a number of follow-up studies began to come to fruition (Nemzek 1933; Thorndike 1933, 1940). From these, two generalizations emerged. First, early measures seldom correlated strongly with later. Second, regardless of age, the longer the time interval, the lower the correlation between assessments. Some years later, the results of the immense Harvard Growth Study were published (Dearborn and Rothney 1941). For both physical and mental growth no two cases (out of hundreds) were found to have exactly the same developmental history. However, although prediction of growth was 'extremely hazardous', children in general tended to remain in the same broad classification between age 8 and 16. Thus, this early work failed to offer support for the thesis that early characteristics, shaped as they are by genetic–environmental interactions, were closely related to later measures. However, the poor standardization of early cognitive measures (e.g. the 1916 and 1937 Stanford–Binet tests) may well in some studies have exaggerated the extent of personal changes over time.

Tracing the development of single characteristics

There are hundreds – perhaps thousands – of studies following different samples from early to later periods of develoment. Here some of the better known research will be sampled. A classic longitudinal study, using data from the Fels Institute, followed children on a variety of single measures from birth to maturity (Kagan and Moss 1962). Here it was only between years six and ten onwards – and not earlier – that significant correlations between childhood personality measures and their adult equivalent were obtained. These correlations were moderate in size, averaging about 0.5. A further important contribution was published by Bloom (1964), which in its title (*Stability and Change in Human Characteristics*) reflected the shift away from an unadulterated constancy model, but over-emphasized the constancies found. However, this study was marred by a notion of 'half-development', in our view a meaningless concept.

In more recent publications much has been made of Block's (1971) *Lives Through Time*. Using a variety of measures coalesced from the Oakland and Berkeley Guidance Studies, Block used a Q-sort technique to track personality development for each individual from Junior to Senior High School and then to adulthood. Average correlations for individuals from Junior to Senior were around 0.75, and for the longer period from Senior to adulthood 0.55. There was a wide range among the sample members in the degree of consistency or change over time. Specifically, a minority remained very constant while at the other extreme some proved to be very different. Bloom and others have highlighted the constancy phenomenon, while others have emphasized the marked differences between the constancies in some, the changes in others, and the mixture of both in the majority (see also Block 1980). MacFarlane (1964), ruminating on the findings of the Berkeley Guidance Study (analysed by Block) with which she had been associated since its inception, wrote:

> Many of our most mature and competent adults had severely troubled and confusing childhoods and adolescences. Many of our highly successful children and adolescents have failed to achieve their predicted potential. One sees among them at age 30 a high proportion of brittle, discontented and puzzled adults whose high potentialities have not been actualized at least as of now ... [but] we

were not always wrong! We did have several small groups whose adult status fulfilled theoretical expectations [i.e. constancy].

Summarizing so far, we have Kagan and Moss and MacFarlane emphasizing changes after earlier development, while Block and Bloom underline constancies. These different interpretations sometimes seem to relate to the expectancies of the researchers. As we have indicated earlier, if you search for constancies you will certainly find them. Similarly, an emphasis on change will be equally rewarded. Only if you seek both will a balanced view be achieved.

One notes also that constancy increases with age. Two early longitudinal studies of IQ, using correlations between three-year assessment intervals, show the following: – ages 3–6, 0.56 and 0.57; ages 5–8, 0.70 and 0.70; ages 7–10, 0.76 and 0.78; and for one study 9–12, 0.85 (Clarke and Clarke 1972).

Bloom (1964), using age 18 scores as a criterion, showed from five different studies closely similar correlations over time, both for IQ and also for scholastic achievement. Once again, the longer the assessment intervals, the lower the correlation (i.e. the greater the change in rank position). Hindley and Owen (1978), using a frequently retested London sample, undertook a sophisticated computer analysis of the varying patterns of development. Seven striking patterns were observed, only one of which represented real constancy.

More recently, using very similar measures across widely different ages, there has been an increasing emphasis on constancy of IQ. Thus Yule, Gold and Busch (1982) assessed Isle of Wight children at five and a half and sixteen and a half with Wechsler tests. A high correlation of 0.86 was obtained, and only 10 per cent of the sample varied by more than 13 points from original scores.

A further example comes from research reported by Moffitt *et al.* (1993). Using a New Zealand sample of 794 children, assessed at ages seven, nine, eleven and thirteen on the WISC-R, these authors suggest that overall IQ change is either negligible in amount, unreliably measured or both. However, a good deal of intra-individual variability occurred. Thus 107 children (13.5% of the sample) showed changes which via cluster analysis could be grouped into six reliable patterns. There were no significant correlates of changes. While this variability was marked, the amount of cumulative and sequential change averaged only 5.3 IQ points across the seven years. Only one of the six patterns showed a monotonic trajectory, that of IQ increment, applying to only 3 per cent of the sample. 'In general, then, patterns of IQ change appear to conform to recovery curves and seem to reflect level-maintaining or even level-seeking phenomena … IQ appears to be elastic rather than plastic' (p.496). These findings surprised the authors, being for them entirely unexpected.

While these last three examples tend to emphasize that only in a minority do sustained, sequential changes take place within relatively constant environments, we wish to underline 'relatively'. Quite significant alterations in children's circumstances do not influence IQ, although they may well impinge on other characteristics. However, where children are rescued from dire circumstances, the situation is entirely different, for gross environmental deprivation may have very marked detrimental effects which in better circumstances may be reversed (Clarke and Clarke 1992).

The predictive value of infant tests has until recently been largely written off (including by ourselves) on the grounds of very low correlation with later IQ due, it has been assumed, to the total lack of correspondence between the content of early and later measures. In addition, growth is so fast in the first year of life that fluctuant abilities may predominate. During the last decade, however, there has been increasing interest in the predictive power of infant information processing, including response to novelty, habituation and other aspects of perception. Correlations as high as 0.61 have been reported (Slater *et al.* 1989) between length of fixation to a novel stimulus at the age of six months and the WISC-R at eight years, although the majority of predictive indices fell well short of this value. (See also Slater (1995) for an overview.)

McCall and Carriger (1993), in their meta-analysis, gave a raw median correlation of 0.45 between habituation and recognition memory assessments in the first year of life and IQ measured at between one and eight years of age. It must be remembered that any sizeable correlation is surprising when we consider the low reliabilities reported for the early measures. There is a degree of controversy surrounding these results. A troubling finding is an association between sample size and predictive correlation. These authors report a -0.60 correlation on the basis of a collation of data assembled by Bornstein and Sigman (1986), and in their own meta-analysis -0.56 for all samples, -0.79 for habituation samples and -0.46 for recognition. It has been suggested that extreme scores, particularly for at-risk infants, might account, at least in part, for the results.

Laucht, Esser and Schmidt (1994) studied a sample of 226 three-month-old infants recorded as 'at risk', using habituation–dishabituation methods of assessment. Cognitive development was assessed at the age of two and four and a half. There was a significant prediction of outcome, as expected, but correlations from the more conventional infant tests such as the Bayley were higher. Many have claimed the superiority of early information-processing over the latter. The authors also found that early biological and social factors better predicted later IQ. Laucht *et al.* attribute the many recently reported higher correlations between the new infant tests and later IQ to small sample sizes, leading to differential publication of high versus low correlations, a suggestion also considered by McCall and Carriger (1993). The debate will continue.

Summarizing so far, recent work on the single characteristic, IQ, suggests that, under normal circumstances and using individual Wechsler tests, relatively accurate *broad* prediction of adolescent IQs may be made around age five. Such predictions become more precise with increasing age. It might be added that educational measures are more variable, and we would remind readers that the IQ was originally designed to predict educational ability. However, in later chapters we shall note that a very different picture emerges from studies of children rescued from adversity.

During the last decade there has been increasing interest in 'basic' personality characteristics, especially shyness. Kagan has been foremost in tracing the development of early shyness (Kagan 1992; Kagan and Snidman 1991). They indicate that even with high heritability, a very substantial minority show phenotypic changes over time. Some who were unusually inhibited as infants were no longer so later, while others earlier uninhibited had later become shy both with adults and other children (Kagan 1992 p.994). Presumably such changes were the result of intervening experiences. The majority of very inhibited children may, however, be at risk of a very introverted adulthood.

A further contribution by Kagan (1997) amplifies the earlier picture, especially his linkage of behavioural characteristics and neuroscience. Around 20 per cent of 462 healthy children, middle-class and 16 weeks old, became active and distressed when presented with brightly coloured toys moved back and forth in front of their faces, tape recordings of voices speaking brief sentences and so forth. In contrast, around 40 per cent were low reactive. When the high and low reactive children were studied in a variety of laboratory situations at 14 and 21 months, around one-third of the high reactives were very fearful and only 3 per cent showed minimal fear. In contrast, one-third of the low reactives were minimally fearful at both ages. What happens later to high and low reactives?

At age four, both sets of children were interviewed, blind to the original rating, by an unfamiliar female examiner. The high reactive children talked and smiled less than did the low reactives. However, only a modest proportion of children maintained an extreme form of their expected profile over the period four months to four and a half years. It was uncommon for either high or low reactive children to develop the seminal features of the other type, but quite common for each to develop a profile characteristic of the less extreme child who is neither very timid nor very bold. In short, this suggests only partial continuity.

A notable addition to the literature on this problem has been provided by Kerr et al. (1994), who carried out on a Swedish longitudinal sample a 'conceptual replication' of Kagan's work. Among questions raised were whether extremes of inhibition showed greater stability over time than non-extremes, and whether there are gender differences in stability. We have ourselves (1988) suggested that extremes are likely to have a different developmental history than others.

Data on a large sample consisted of mothers' ratings over a 16-year period, and psychologists' ratings over the first six years of life. The former was concerned with perceived shyness towards strangers, and the latter with inhibited behaviour in the testing situation. On the question of temporal stability for the whole group, the findings reflected the two principles to which we have drawn attention over several decades. Correlations increase with increasing age, and the longer the time gap between assessments, the lower the correlation (i.e. the greater the likelihood of change in individual ordinal position). In the context of the present theme, the greatest interest is in whether there are differences in stability between those at the extremes of the distribution versus those in the non-extreme group. For the first six years, stability data supported Kagan's findings. However, 'behaviour did change in the long run ... For most of our subjects the early causes of extremely inhibited or uninhibited behaviour were not long-lasting' (Kerr *et al.* 1994, p.144). Although ratings were more stable for children in the extreme groups, stability into adolescence was only found for inhibited females. Here the authors speculate that culturally shared notions of gender-appropriate behaviour influences the stability of inhibition. This, then, is a study that emphasizes for many of the sample a relative long-term unpredictability of personality characteristics. We must be aware, however, that overt behaviour may cover up internal inhibitions, and that self-awareness of our own personality may lead to compensatory overt behaviour (Chess and Thomas 1984). For a useful overview, see Plomin and Dunn (1986).

A further report by Kerr, Lambert and Bem (1996) adds interesting information. Using age 35 data from the longitudinal study compared with the mother-rated shyness at age 8–10, shy Swedish boys married and became fathers later than non-shy boys. Unlike American findings, however, their adult careers were unaffected by their temperamental characteristics. The shy Swedish girls, like their American counterparts, married later and became mothers at the same time as their peers. However, their educational levels were lower than those of the non-shy girls. The authors once again point out that the life consequences of shyness depend upon its culturally defined gender and situation appropriateness. For example, Americans tend to devalue shyness while Swedes do not.

Using information from the Berkeley Guidance Study, Caspi, Elder and Bem (1988) followed up a group of late childhood shy children at ages 30 and 40. Very significant associations were found, especially for men, with delayed marriage, delayed fatherhood, as well as entry to a stable career. The authors indicate the likelihood that childhood shyness leads to avoidance of novel situations, particularly at life transitions, and point to the reciprocal person/environmental dynamics which can maintain behaviour. Although the differences between adult outcomes of shy and non-shy children are often striking, the data make clear that predictions from late childhood are imperfect, with overlaps between these groups. It would be important to know the mechanisms for individual predictive failure. This study is very important in view of the late childhood baseline, a time when in many cases shyness would have become habitual, and also in the very lengthy follow-up to early middle age.

Of course, shyness in early childhood may have somewhat different origins and functions compared with later childhood onset or adult shyness. However, this field of research confirms the general findings on other characteristics. There are large individual differences in the degree of constancy or relative change over time.

A similar picture emerges from the New York Longitudinal Study (Thomas and Chess 1976, 1977) of 136 subjects from infancy to adolescence, which will be mentioned in the next section. Correlations over time for nine separate baby characteristics were not impressive. Only when some of these were combined were there signs of important constancies.

Tracing the development of broader characteristics

Tracing the longitudinal assessment of broader characteristics (e.g. emotional stability/instability) might be assumed to reveal greater constancies over time than can occur for narrower, single processes. Within the broad, the fluctuant narrower components may be sub-merged in the overall measure. For example, in Hilda Lewis's (1954) pioneering study (see Chapters One and Five) a general psychiatric rating was employed. The children, who were among the most deprived in Kent, were (modal age, 8–11) assessed psychiatrically before being allotted to varying forms of care. On admission 40 per cent were in fair or good condition. Two years later this had increased to 75 per cent. So here the samples exhibited substantial constancies as well as significant change. Moreover, the new situations in which these children found themselves represented late interventions.

The Terman Study, Oden's (1968) 40-year follow-up of Terman's gifted children in middle age, used broad characterization of the 100 most successful (A group) and the 100 least successful male adults, the

C group. On education, 34 per cent of the A group and only 1 per cent of the C group had achieved PhDs or other doctorates. In occupational status 99 per cent of the A group were either professional or managerial, as against 18 per cent of the C group. This study is interesting as showing the divergence of extremes from the original fairly homogeneous childhood categorization as extremely gifted. They underline Dearborn and Rothney's (1941) view that prediction of development is hazardous. (Note, however, that for some types of child disorder, early prediction is very accurate.)

Abnormalities and their development

There is a vast literature on prediction from child or adolescent abnormal personality, with some hundreds of longitudinal studies (see, for example, Mednick and Baert 1981). Here we examine just a few. Rodgers (1990) used a 36-year follow-up of a national birth cohort to study the associations between childhood behaviour and personality with affective disorder. The adult criterion was the Present State Examination. The author regards the accuracy of prediction as unimpressive (p.411), but in a few instances the prognosis was especially poor, notably for bed-wetting frequency at age six, frequent truanting at age fifteen and speech problems at the same age. Even the identification of groups with multiple risk factors failed to yield a high number of cases.

Another study which repays close reading has been reported by Esser, Schmidt and Woerner (1990) in Germany. In a rather brief longitudinal account of a large cohort of 365 children, randomly selected between the ages of eight and thirteen, around 16 per cent at age eight exhibited moderate or severe psychiatric disorders. The same percentage was found at age thirteen, but the distribution of diagnoses at this later age had changed substantially, with a remarkable increase in conduct disorders, with similar rates for girls as for boys. For us, the most interesting finding was the fairly common switch from no disorders at age eight to disorders at age thirteen, and from disorders at age eight to no disorders at age thirteen. Specifically, one half of the disordered eight-year-olds were similarly rated at thirteen, while half were not. Adverse family situations and learning disabilities were associated with new conduct disorders, but more accurate prediction for emotional disorders were the number of life events and adverse family situations. At one extreme, three-quarters of those with conduct disorders at age eight were persistently disordered at age thirteen, but, at the other, early neurotic disorders were likely to remit. Such findings are amply supported by previous work.

We now turn to studies of children who showed less severe but worrying adjustment difficulties and disorders that are usually defined as maladaptive reactions to psychosocial stressors leading to impairment of functioning, or symptoms that are in excess of normal reactions. These include severe anxiety, sleep disturbances, phobias and depression, identified at different periods of childhood and adolescence. How do they fare in adult life? The answer, by contrast with many other psychiatric disorders, is *well*.

As with many abnormal conditions, adjustment disorders may arise from a variety of different, and sometimes overlapping, causes. There are a number of obvious variables: the family context, especially the quality of parenting; the degree of match or mismatch between parents and between parents and child; the qualities of individual vulnerability and resilience during or following stress; the enhanced probability of disorder in those with organic brain dysfunction (e.g. Rutter and Sandberg 1985); the doubled risk of emotional and conduct disorders in inner-city areas (London) compared with rural areas (Isle of Wight).

The New York Longitudinal Study, initiated in 1956 by Chess and Thomas (and referred to earlier), provides a careful prospective longitudinal study of childhood disorders, uniquely with data gathered in all cases before onset (Chess and Thomas 1984; Thomas *et al.* 1968). The sample consisted of 133 middle- to upper-middle-class subjects recruited through personal contact with parents during pregnancy or shortly after birth. An important incentive for joining the study and remaining in it was the promise of free high-quality medical care. There was no attrition among the 133 children whose families joined.

Adjustment disorders represent a wide range of very common behavioural problems, which, as Chess and Thomas note, in many cases represent age-specific behaviour that, though troublesome, are not suggestive of pathological deviation. Sometimes the issue is simple, involving inappropriateness of the routines employed by parents. Suggesting alternative ways of handling the child can be effective. When problems are not resolved, psychiatric evaluation and sometimes treatment are necessary. As is to be expected in this sample, there were virtually no conduct disorders. Of forty-five clinical cases in childhood, forty exhibited adjustment disorders, the majority classified as mild. By adolescence twenty-four had recovered and two had improved; by adulthood twenty-nine had recovered and five had improved their original childhood diagnostic status, two were unchanged, two were moderately worse, and two were markedly worse. In additon, of twelve cases with onset during adolescence, six were completely recovered in early adult life, including three with severe problems (Chess and Thomas 1984).

Chess and Thomas had first identified nine different categories of infantile temperament, each of which later proved to have rather poor predictive quality. Combined into three different, broad groups, however, a much better prediction of behavioural risk became apparent. These groups were 'The Easy Child', 'The Difficult Child' and 'The Slow-to-Warm-Up Child', each being very carefully defined. Not all children in the sample were accounted for in these categories, nor did particular individuals necessarily remain within their group. But the greater risk of *later* disorder (70%) lay in the 'Difficult' children. But as implied in the paragraph above, prospects in adolescence and early adult life for these *mildly* reactive behaviour disorders were good. Here the 'goodness of fit' concept (see Chapter One) was helpful both in understanding and remediating early problems (Chess and Thomas 1984, 1999).

Two recent prospective longitudinal studies, one from Sweden (Von Knorring, Andersson and Magnusson 1987) and one from Germany, already mentioned (Esser *et al.* 1990), confirm the fade-out of clinically diagnosed adjustment disorders with time. The Von Knorring *et al.* study provided data on a large, representative sample, prospectively from 10 to 24 years and retrospectively from 0 to 9 years. In reviewing relevant literature these authors noted the higher incidence of childhood disorders in cities, compared with towns and rural areas, and the higher incidence in boys than girls, which, however, is reversed during adolescence. Conduct disorders may be dealt with other than clinically, but the authors underline the poor prognosis for these, with good outcomes for children with emotional disorders.

The criteria for inclusion in the Von Knorring *et al.* (1987) sample were different from those in the Chess and Thomas research, as the former depended on the rather tough criterion of psychiatric referral during childhood through early adulthood. The findings endorse other work, however; only 3 of 28 children exhibiting anxiety and emotional disorders before 9 years of age remained in psychiatric care in early adulthood, whereas a quarter of a large group with onset at 10 to 14 years and almost half of those with onset between 15 and 19 years were still in psychiatric care between ages 20 and 24. Males who had attended special classes were at particular risk for developing these disorders.

Early social disadvantages

A related topic concerns the life path of children removed from problem families. Two studies reported by Quinton *et al.* (1982) complement one another and illustrate, as noted earlier, an important principle. Prospective and retrospective studies on the same theme and with similar populations yield somewhat different answers to the same question (see Chapter Two). A major reason is that an identified adult deviant group may enable a continuous deviant past history to be revealed in a retrospective investigation, *whereas there is no way of knowing how many had similar early histories yet escaped unscathed.* The research by Quinton *et al.* has a bearing on both intra-individual and intergenerational constancy and change.

Both projects studied current parenting and associated psychiatric problems, relating these to past and present circumstances. The authors sought to assess the effects on child rearing of early emotional deprivation, as predicted by early learning theorists (Quinton *et al.* 1982). The first, a retrospective study, evaluated histories of parents whose children had been removed from home and placed in residential care. The second, a prospective study, examined the adult outcome of children originally assessed by the late Jack Tizard and colleagues in the 1960s when they were in residential care, having been themselves removed from home. In both investigations, appropriate carefully chosen comparison groups were used. Important differences emerged between the findings of these two studies: '… our data … show that the picture of intergenerational continuities looking forwards is quite different from that looking backwards' (Quinton *et al.* 1982, p.293). See also Chapter Two.

The retrospective sample of adults with children in care exhibited a strong link between their parenting breakdown and their own adverse childhood experiences; however, comparison group data showed that quite severe early adversities seldom led directly to such problems. Thus, an additional linking mechanism must be invoked in the former sample. Multiple personal and material circumstances seem to have been involved (see also Quinton and Rutter 1984a, 1984b).

The second prospective sample of adults who as *children* had been assessed in care indicated that the experience of serious adversities in childhood or of seriously maladaptive and disruptive parenting does not always lead to parenting and other breakdown in the next generation. There is certainly an increased 'risk' but this is not a 'probability'. Many comparison children had also experienced severe adversity but had survived. Indeed, 'intergenerational discontinuities outweigh continuities' (Quinton *et al.* 1982, p.293). Nearly a third of the women, removed from their parents and reared in institutions, showed good parenting, and a further quarter displayed only moderate difficulties of a type also shown by 40 per cent of the comparison group (for an overview, see Rutter, Quinton and Liddle 1983).

The general point here is that early adversity can set up a chain of consequences. The effects of early adversity can produce new environmental effects; there also appears to be an increased personal vulnerability to later adversity. Later events in adolescence or adulthood can be potent agents of amelioration or added difficulties. For example, indirect selective factors may lead to choosing a stable and supportive marriage partner or an unstable, equally damaged spouse. Once again, the cumulative and transactional nature of development is implied by these important findings. One small sub-group showed up as particularly vulnerable (Rutter *et al.* 1983). Ten children had been admitted to institutional care before the age of two years and had remained there continuously until sixteen years of age or older, inevitably experiencing the relatively detached, multiple-person caretaking that characterize institutions. Eight of the ten showed later problems, and although this sub-group difference fell short of statistical significance, it is possible that detached, multiple-person caretaking commencing in infancy may be as unsatisfactory in its consequences as rearing in seriously discordant multi-problem situations.

Many other studies show that there are always some children who escape the dire predictions suggested by their early circumstances. In 1972, Sir Keith Joseph initiated what became known as the Transmitted Deprivation Programme. He had asked why it was that in spite of major social improvements since the end of World War II, 'deprivation and problems of adjustment so conspicuously persist? ... social attitudes and ways of life tend to recur in some families from one generation to the next. But what is more surprising [is that] this does not always happen' (Brown and Madge 1982). In *Cycles of Disadvantage* (Rutter and Madge 1976) and *Despite the Welfare State* (Brown and Madge 1982) the field was reviewed at the beginning and end of the programme, respectively. The 23 studies supported, and the more than a dozen commissioned reviews of relevant world literature endorsed, the view that cycles of deprivation do exist but do not inevitably recur between generations. There is both escape from, and recruitment to, deprivation. These books offer a very comprehensive account of the problem under discussion (see also Chapter Five).

The National Child Development Study (NCDS) has followed the development of all children born in the United Kingdom during one week in March 1958. Various sub-samples, as well as the whole cohort, have been the subject of separate analyses. Here the study of only one sub-sample is mentioned.

In *Born to Fail?* Wedge and Prosser (1973) underlined data on 11-year-olds in the NCDS, the already robust findings concerning the physical and psychological correlates of socio-economic status. They had a widespread impact, drawing public attention to

> the massive accumulation of burdens afflicting disadvantaged children and their families, and which they are frequently expected somehow to overcome. Yet it should cause no surprise that so many of these children fail to 'behave', fail to 'learn' and fail to succeed ... one in sixteen, the disadvantaged group, suffered adversity after adversity, heaped upon them from before birth; their health was poorer, their school attainment lower and their physical environment worse in almost every way than that of ordinary children. (p.59)

So the question for the future becomes, did they all fail in later development?

Fortunately, this study was continued by Essen and Wedge (1982), as part of the Transmitted Deprivation series. It concerned children in the NCDS who were identified as socially disadvantaged at 11, 16, or both 11 and 16. These data, together with earlier information, were designed to represent the ecology of these children at different stages of development. One of the main aims was to determine whether families experience long-term or transitory difficulties, and how these bear on outcome. Such families could at the same time be compared with ordinary families.

The criteria of disadvantage were threefold: rearing in atypical families, poor housing or low income. At ages 11 and 16, the percentages for the whole NCDS sample were, for the first criterion, 19.8 and 19.3; for the second, 14.7 and 10.2; and for the third, 13.1 and 11.9, respectively. Those who fulfilled all three criteria at age 11 constituted 4.5 per cent, but by age 16 this had declined to 2.9 per cent. Although the findings show some continuities between ages 11 and 16, marked discontinuities were also evident. Of all the disadvantaged at either age, about a quarter were disadvantaged at both ages, half at age 11 only, and a quarter at age 16 only. It is therefore clear that a larger group suffered disadvantage at some stage in childhood than is indicated by the cross-sectional findings at ages 11 and 16 (Essen and Wedge 1982, p.46). This underlines the fact that even an extreme ecology is not necessarily static. From the detailed findings, it became clear that those who at 11 or 16 years were multiply disadvantaged were found to show poorer achievement and behaviour and to be shorter on average than ordinary children.

Multiple disadvantages at either age were equally damaging to the children's life chances. It is of interest that for outcome measures at age 16, those who were multiply disadvantaged at that age were at no greater disadvantage than those who had experienced such problems at age 11. 'Neither of these ages appears to be particularly critical ... [in] that multiple disadvantage of either, and therefore perhaps any, age is equally damaging to the children's life chances' (Essen and Wedge 1982, p.166). More recently, a further NCDS group was followed up with interviews at age 26/27 of an educationally successful sample and a comparison group, both of whom had been disadvantaged during one or more periods in childhood. The former were somewhat less disadvantaged than the latter, and certain parental and adolescent aspirations for the future seemed relevant. It was already known that such qualities as easy temperament and good motivation were relevant to escape. This final study confirmed the importance of such factors, and indicated that the achievers had better relationships in their homes than did the comparison subjects. The strongest predictors related to parental interest in the child's education, and, of course, educational achievement is the key to a better adult life (Pilling 1990).

Childhood sexual abuse

There is a vast literature on this serious problem, recently highlighted by a Home Office Report, *Sex Offending against Children: Understanding the Risk* (1999), which indicates that 72,600 children are abused each year. This is regarded as a considerable underestimate. Of course, such abuse is not confined to the very early years, but can take place at any childhood or adolescent age. There is a widespread belief that psychological consequences are inevitable, understandable in the light of the incidents themselves and the probable type of ongoing family context in which they occur.

There is a problem with several of the published studies, common to much research into causal factors in later abnormal behaviour. These start from the recognized atypical behaviour and look back to find what might be relevant in the case histories. This strategy is to some extent flawed because it does not allow for those unknown number of people, with similar factors in their childhood background, who *do not* grow into atypical adults. Those seriously affected may not be wholly representative of *all* cases of childhood sexual abuse. Three recent studies illustrate this point. First, two studies by Mullen *et al.* (1993, 1994). A postal questionnaire was sent to 2250 New Zealand women and very detailed information was obtained from a wide range of questions. From the responses to the questionnaires, two groups were selected for detailed interviews. The first involved 298 women who had reported childhood sexual abuse; the second, another 298 who did not so report.

While a history of child sexual abuse was associated with increased risk of psychiatric problems 'it should not be overlooked that many victims gave no account of significant psychiatric difficulties' (Mullen *et al.* 1993, p.728). The authors go on to state: 'The overlap between the possible effects of sexual abuse and the effects of the matrix of social disadvantage ... were so considerable as to raise doubts about how often, in practice, it operates as an independent causal element.' The 1994 report indicated that only 53.8 per cent of the women attributed long term effects directly to the abuse. Where such effects were present, they included lack of trust, fear of men, damage to self-esteem and self-confidence, and in some cases sexual problems. These could sometimes be indirect effects and therefore potentially preventable.

Turning to the other half of the problem, there is a widespread belief that perpetrators of child sexual abuse have themselves inevitably been abused as children. If this were so, then very precise predictions might be made. Again, there may have been a reporting bias leading to such beliefs. An important three-year Scottish study by Waterhouse, Dobash and Carnie (1994) indicates, among other things, that the conventional view is simplistic and incorrect.

The first part of the study considered around 500 cases of child sexual abuse, but was marred by the uneven amount of information available on the childhood backgrounds of the abusers. The second part of the research is much more revealing about our theme, that the abused do not necessarily become abusers.

It used one- to two-hour skilled, in-depth interviews with 53 abusers, mainly in prison, a reasonably representative sample of this population. A large amount of important information emerged. Here we note only that almost half described their childhood as 'unhappy'. Offences of the abusers were either classified as 'familial' (48%) or 'extra-familial' (52%). The childhood backgrounds of the latter group were generally quite different from those abusing within the family. They were more likely to have grown up in disrupted families in which significant parental violence towards them was noted, or where a parental mental health problem existed. Those who abused from outside the victim's family were more likely to have experienced prolonged separations or to have grown up in institutions. They were much more likely to have suffered sexually abusive behaviour as children than were those who had abused members of their own families. However, of the total sample of abusers interviewed (53) only 22 (41%) reported early sexual abuse, while 31 did not. As noted, the former tended to come from more disrupted families than those who had not so suffered. (A useful review which, however, does not include reference to Mullen *et al.* (1994) nor Waterhouse, Dobash and Carnie (1994) has been provided by Hilton and Mezey 1996.)

The findings of this study confirm, yet again, that for complex behaviour, the search for single causes is unlikely to be successful. In this, as in other fields, there exists a web of interrelated factors which indicate probabilities of varying strengths, not certainties. The view that abusers have *inevitably* been themselves abused is here shown to be incorrect.

Summary

Examples have been given of the development of single characteristics such as IQ, responses to novelty, and shyness under natural circumstances in which it can be assumed that no major environmental changes took place. The general picture was one of constancies in some individuals and changes in others, the amounts of the latter depending on the measures used, the particular samples and the characteristic in question. If early development were predeterministic, then constancy should be very strong, especially when reinforced by relatively unchanging conditions. Early characteristics are, however, poorly correlated with their adult equivalents.

Turning to broader characteristics, a brief account of the outcome for Terman's group of gifted children was offered, followed by more lengthy summaries of abnormal development, early social disadvantage and the outcome of child sexual abuse. Once again, one is struck by the failure of early measures strongly to predict outcome. There are, of course, many exceptions (e.g. autism, severe learning problems or conduct disorders), but one way in which early adversity can lead to a very poor outcome is when one unfortunate happening leads to another in a chain reaction. Even so, there will always be some who escape their apparent destiny. Acknowledging that certain environments pose risks in development, Magnusson (1991) supplies a useful corrective in stating that 'most people from a particular environment do not become criminals or abusers of alcohol. In fact, many of the people who make constructive, highly useful contributions to society are from the very environments believed to predestine social maladjustment' (pp.1–2).

CHAPTER FOUR

Children Rescued from Very Severe Adversity

Signpost: *Good outcome for very severely deprived children after strong intervention*

Following the fortunes of children rescued from the most severe conditions of privation represents the toughest test of our thesis. Are they damaged for life even though in better conditions? If not, do they remain somewhat impaired? A number of case studies, as well as research on groups, will answer these questions.

For many centuries there have been stories of children reared by animals, the so-called feral children. In one or two cases these have been pure invention, but in most they represent the attempt of unsophisticated people to account for children acting very abnormally and found wandering in forests or jungle. Most writers now suggest that such children had been recently abandoned on account of their abnormalities. With the contemporary presence of wild animals, a spurious connection was assumed. In brief, there is no authenticated account of any child having been reared by animals (but see Malson (1972) for a more sympathetic interpretation).

There are, however, one or two indications of attempts to treat such 'captured' children, the best known of which was reported in the early nineteenth century by J.M.G. Itard. There can be little doubt that this child was autistic and that he had been wandering in the Aveyron woods for several years. Itard had 'Victor' fostered and conducted sophisticated learning experiments on him. The boy improved socially, but remained very severely impaired.

Then there is the mysterious case of Kaspar Hauser, found in 1828 outside the gates of Nuremberg. This young man gave an account of lifelong isolation under the care of a guardian. He obtained a clerical post, but after receiving a message telling him that he would be given the secret of his origin, went to a rendezvous and was later found there murdered (Malson 1972).

There are several more recent biographies, one of which strikes us as so riddled with improbabilities as to be scarcely worth recording. In this case, an attempt to make contact with the Spanish author via his publisher came to nothing. However, an autobiography (written jointly with his therapist) of a young man kept prisoner by his sadistic mother, often chained to a radiator or locked in a large cupboard over a period of eight years, rings true (Bisson and De Schonen 1994). Although his hands were deliberately badly burned by his mother, and his emotional life wrecked until he escaped when aged 12, he has made a considerable recovery, and now works as a waiter in Paris.

There are, however, modern studies which are unmysterious, and often well reported. To varying extents their earlier histories prior to isolatation were known. Deranged parents or grandparents put these children into prolonged conditions which must have even threatened their survival. The first modern account was given by Kingsley Davis (1940, 1947). These children, Anna and Isabelle, were discovered separately and at about the same time, both being aged about six. Anna received no specialist treatment and her general level of functioning, though showing improvement, remained severely retarded up to the time when she died at the age of ten and a half years from haemorrhagic jaundice. The well-known case of Genie (Curtiss 1977) is another where organic impairment is suspected, and where improvement from an autistic-like condition was very limited.

The illegitimate Isabelle and her deaf-mute mother were imprisoned in an attic. The child was severely malnourished, rachitic and without speech. After discovery she received specialist speech therapy, and the changes in her were rapid and remarkable. It is important that this case was independently reported upon by Mason (1942), who was in charge of the girl's speech remediation. It is a great pity that the authors were unable to discover very much about the parentage of these girls; little was known about paternity. Nor is there any exact indication of the emotional state of Isabelle when followed up finally at age 14. Educationally, she was then apparently a little below average, but in general was considered normal. We do not know whether she herself had memories of her early years, or of her responsiveness to a radical change of environment (as had, for example, Helen Keller). But the case is sufficiently well documented to make it clear that Isabelle showed substantial recovery to normality from a level of severe retardation. Moreover, deprivation of language experience during the normal period of development of this function did not prove to be critical. It is of interest that Lenneberg (1967), basing his views on a wealth of experimental evidence, is cautious in qualifying his conclusion that 'we may speak of a critical period for language acquisition' (p.174). But his concept is very wide: 'Between the ages of three and the early teens the possibility for primary language acquisition continues to be good ... After puberty, the ability for self-organisation and adjustment to the physiological demands of verbal behaviour quickly declines' (p.158). Thus the data presented by Davis, and later in this section by Koluchová, can certainly be accommodated within Lenneberg's (as opposed to narrower and less sophisticated) concepts of critical periods for language. What is surprising, however, in the light of the traditional model of the role of early development, is that barren early experience (though in the company of a deaf-mute mother, of unknown intelligence) had not set for Isabelle an irreversible path.

The best known, most detailed and lengthiest study is by Koluchová (1972, 1976, 1991), and since we had the privilege of bringing these findings to the notice of the English speaking world, we have had the advantage of further information from the author. In its barest outline the facts are as follows.

Identical twin boys, born in 1960, lost their mother shortly after birth, were cared for by a social agency for a year and then fostered by a maternal aunt for a further six months. Their development was normal. Their father, who may have had intellectual limitations, remarried, but his new wife proved to be excessively cruel to the twins, banishing them to the cellar for the next five and a half years and beating them from time to time. Neighbours were frightened of this woman, and were aware that all was not well. On discovery at the age of seven, the twins were dwarfed in stature, lacking speech, suffering from rickets and failing to understand the meaning of pictures. The doctors who examined them confidently predicted permanent physical and mental handicap. Legally removed from their parents, they first underwent a programme of physical remediation, and initially entered a school for children with severe learning disabilities. After some time they were legally adopted by exceptionally dedicated women. Scholastically, from a state of profound disability they caught up with age peers and achieved emotional and intellectual normality. After basic education they went on to technical school, training as typewriter mechanics, but later undertook further education, specializing in electronics. Both were drafted for national service, and later married and had children. They are said to be entirely stable, lacking abnormalities and enjoying warm relationships. One is a computer technician and the other a technical training instructor.

The case histories of these two boys bear some resemblance to the account of Isabelle. All three were rachitic on discovery at ages six and seven; and all three lacked speech. Isabelle's initially very low IQ trebled in 18 months, while the twins' mental ages increased from three to eight years within two years of discovery, and IQs from 40 to 95 and 93 in four years, a slower rate of recovery. As adults, the twins' IQs stabilized at around 115. All three cases had experienced prolonged privation, yet with strong intervention this had not predestined them to a permanent condition of severe handicap.

In addition to single case studies, there are other records of groups of children rescued form severe privation. Freud and Dann (1951), reporting an observational study on the first six children rescued from the concentration camp at Tereszin and brought to Britain in 1945, ascribe much importance to peer relations. All had been orphaned at 12 months or earlier and reared by a succession of concentration camp inmates until aged about three. In a one-year follow-up it was clear that they were hypersensitive, restless, aggressive and difficult to handle,

> but they were neither deficient, delinquent nor psychotic. They … had mastered some of their anxieties, and developed social attitudes. That they were able to acquire a new language in the midst of their upheavals, bears witness to a basically unharmed contact with their environment.

This is attributed to the relations these children had formed with one another in the camp. Their feelings towards one another 'show a warmth and spontaneity which is unheard of in ordinary relations between young contemporaries'. The same point has been made by Koluchová.

Similarly, Rathbun, DiVirgilio and Waldfogel (1958) briefly reviewed the work of Bowlby and Spitz, and believed that their evidence of the adverse effects of early deprivation was impressive. Nevertheless, since the studies were for the most part retrospective, the investigators were in no position to evaluate what attempts were made at rehabilitating these children. They believed:

> ... knowing the severe traumata to which the children had been exposed, one would expect that special ameliorative measures would be needed to counteract their destructive effects. There is no evidence that such measures were undertaken in any of the studies reported. Until one explores this possibility, it is premature to conclude that these effects of severe, early deprivation are irreversible. (1958, p.40)

The authors were fortunate in having a remarkable opportunity to observe the beginnings of the restitutive process in a group of young children brought to the United States under the Inter-Country Adoption Program set up by the Refugee Relief Act of 1953. These thirty-eight young children were placed directly in their permanent adoptive homes, and there could be no gradual transition period as normally favoured by adoption agencies. They were allocated in advance to their prospective homes, and the necessary legal steps were taken. The child travelled by plane and met his or her new parents at the airport, where social and children's workers were present to give as much support as possible. During the initial period the social worker kept in touch by telephone and by personal visits.

Thirty-three families took the thirty-eight children; one family took three siblings and three took two children each. Only fourteen of the families had no children of their own. At the time of arrival the refugees ranged in age from five months to ten years; there were an equal number of boys and girls. Many were illegitimate and others were foundlings whose age, background and early history were unknown. Greece and Korea were the countries sending most children, and others were of Japanese, Italian, Armenian, Austrian or mixed parentage. Little or no information was available regarding early mothering experiences and nearly all had been in institutions for varying lengths of time. In Korea, particularly, the plight of illegitimate children was so desperate that the main problem was keeping them alive rather than of meeting other less pressing needs.

A record was kept of the child's behaviour from the time he or she arrived at the airport. Particularly during the early period, a detailed note was made of the intensity and duration of these responses to cultural transplantation. It must be remembered, for example, that none of the children knew any English, although a few of the adoptive parents were able to talk to the children in their own language. At the airport, some cried and struggled, while others seemed passive. In the new homes the most common problems were overeating and sleep disturbance. Bedtime in particular seemed to reactivate the fears of separation which ran through all age groups, and many needed the presence of the adoptive mother until they went to sleep. Nightmares occurred often, especially among the older children.

Among the children who were toilet-trained on arrival, there were no cases of serious regression. Several Korean children showed fear of the bathroom because of lack of familiarity with its use. Most of the children reacted to their changed life by making excessive demands on their new parents. They would often cling, solicit demonstrations of love, and express resentment of the presence of their new siblings. While many appeared sad on arrival, there were only four cases out of the thirty-eight where this continued long enough to justify a diagnosis of reactive depression. This is indeed remarkable in view of the radical changes which they had undergone, and as the authors write, 'the outstanding feature of this group of children is their almost incredible resiliency' (Rathbun *et al.* 1958, p.412).

An attempt was made to employ a three-point rating for initial reactions of the children; these were termed mild where there was little evidence of disturbance or where there might be an initial acute reaction which disappeared within a week or two; where intensity was great, duration long and the effects pervading the whole personality, the reactions were regarded as severe; and moderate reactions were those occurring between these two extremes. Only eight out of 38 (about 20%) were regarded as severe, with about 40 per cent moderate and another 40 per cent mild. The authors consider that a major factor limiting these initial reactions was the understanding and help given by the adoptive parents. For example, there were only two severe reactions in the twenty-four children below the age of four years; yet this is the age range which other investigators have believed to be the most vulnerable. In fact, however, persistent difficulties were more common in the older children and seemed usually to have preceded their adoptive placement.

The authors recognized that the fact that most had quickly re-established their mental equilibrium did not necessarily imply that they had worked through the disturbing emotions connected with the disruptions they had experienced, but there was evidence that their adjustment was not merely a surface one. Almost without exception they acquired English with remarkable speed, and they made excellent school progress, with not a single case of serious learning disability. Most impressive was the fact that with only a few exceptions the children did not seem to be suffering from either the emotional 'freezing' or the indiscriminate friendliness described by Bowlby. The authors indicated that later developmental crises might possibly reactivate difficulties, but also pointed out that the degree of recovery then observed could never have been predicted from the classic writers on deprivation. They did not reiterate, however, that in many cases these children had little to be *separated from*, and this surely is relevant. But, as they wrote, their data indicated that 'for the child suffering extreme loss, the chances of recovery are far better than had previously been expected'. They added that selective factors clearly operated in the adoptive parents, in their readiness to accept a foreign child with little or no history, and that the children, too, for a variety of reasons, may have been better endowed or may have experienced close relationships in the chaos of their early existence. Finally, the authors challenge Bowlby's (1951) statement that 'good mothering is almost useless if delayed until after the age of two and a half years', and believe that their results are of special significance in an era where rupture of family ties is so common.

A follow-up of this group has been provided by Rathbun *et al.* (1965), six years after arrival in the United States. With the exception of five children whose adoptive families had moved, the complete sample was restudied. The findings were primarily based upon semi-structured interviews with the adoptive families, conducted by an experienced caseworker not previously with them. With parental consent, additional information was obtained from schools in 26 cases. A two-part rating scale was developed, referring to 12 factors comprising personal competence, home, school and community relationships. Independently, the four authors rated each case, and after discussion these were reconciled as a pooled evaluation. Ages at the time of interview ranged from six to sixteen years. Findings indicated that these children were placed in better-than-average American homes and were possessed of better-than-average personal assets. On average they were physically very healthy, of above average IQ, and socially competent. Adjustment for the majority was judged adequate and in some cases notably superior. Specifically, five children were classified as possessing superior adjustment; sixteen were considered adequate; ten were viewed as having a problematic adjustment. The two remaining children were rated as clinically disturbed and in need of professional help.

The authors indicate, however, that current problems could be attributed as readily to the emotional climate of the adoptive home as to the trauma of their early experiences. Of course, many of the children, in their pre-adoptive lives, had shown an ability to tolerate stress, and their adoptive homes, too, were selected as older and 'more established' than the typical couples who adopt American children. Nevertheless, as the authors write, the description earlier given of 'almost incredible resiliency' which characterized their adjustment in the first year in adoptive homes is still applicable to 21 of the 33 children. 'The evidence,' they write, 'points in the direction of a considerable degree of reversibility of the early psychic damage.'

Moskowitz (1985) followed a few of the Holocaust children into adult life. While earlier there had been the view that such children would have been irreparably damaged, 'What now became apparent ... was the wide range of adaptation when there was theoretically no reason to see anything positive ... Many made adaptations that are not only impressive but inspiring' (p.407). As in the Rathbun *et al.* (1965) study, it is significant that the author writes from a psychoanalytical background.

A useful review of most known and properly recorded individual cases (nine in number at that time) has been provided by Skuse (1984). Certain clinical features in such isolated children are, on discovery, virtually ubiquitous: motor retardation, absent or rudimentary language, grossly retarded perceptuomotor skills, paucity of emotional expression, lack of attachment behaviour, and social withdrawal. If recovery is to occur, progress must be rapid at first. Skuse concludes that

> in the absence of genetic or congenital anomalies … victims of such deprivation have an excellent prognosis. Some subtle deficits in social adjustment may persist – most human characteristics, with the possible exception of language, are strongly 'canalised' … and hence virtually resistant to obliteration by even the most dire environments. (p.567)

Subsequent case studies endorse Skuse's view. Thus Thompson (1986, and personal communication 1990) has published the case history of a little boy called Adam who was abandoned at the age of four months in Colombia and brought up in isolation in a reformatory for girls, where she first saw him. The conditions were appalling and the child was severely malnourished. He was removed to an orphanage at 16 months, at which time he weighed only 12 lb 12 oz (i.e. less than 6000 g). Emotionally he was completely withdrawn. He could not sit, walk or crawl. Adam was diagnosed as an extremely malnourished, mentally retarded spastic. Gradually he improved and, at 32 months, was adopted by a North American family, along with a little girl from the same orphanage. Initially, of course, there were problems. Adam was doubly incontinent and frequently bit his sister, but he has continued to improve in his adoptive family and, at age eight, his WISC-R was 113; his sister, who was less severely deprived, had an IQ of 102 at the same age. Both graduated from high school and are emotionally stable. Their physical catch-up was equally impressive.

The clear message, so far, is that conditions of gross deprivation, resulting in physical and mental deficits, can be overcome, provided strong and prolonged interventions take place. It must not be thought that these are achieved without difficulty; far from it. The damaged child not only has to unlearn maladaptive behaviour, but also to learn entirely new forms, sometimes catching up almost from scratch earlier omitted aspects of development. It requires supreme dedication to rear such damaged children.

References here should also be made to a most important study by Rutter *et al.* (1998). This will be reviewed in detail later in Chapter Six. Suffice it to say that a large group of severely deprived Romanian orphans, adopted in the UK before the age of two years and followed up at age four, showed relatively rapid average recovery. Developmental quotients on arrival showed, on average, mild learning disablement which by age four caught up to within the normal range. However, those adopted before age six months improved more that those adopted above this age, and this is unlikely to have arisen from selective factors favouring the younger children (see pp.89–95).

Before proceeding further, a cautionary note must be expressed. Let us suppose that responsive children are more likely to be reported than those who fail to respond to intervention. The unusually large sample referred to above has been followed to six years by O'Connor *et al.* (1999a). A very wide range of cognitive outcomes is reported at this age, including some whose responses to adoptive intervention were limited, with others whose progress was outstanding. Thus, there may be a bias in reporting of single case studies and hence an overestimate of resilience. This can be checked by examining the outcome for large groups of less severely deprived children placed in better situations. They should show the same sort of recovery processes as those we have recorded, but of lesser amount since their earlier problems were less severe. The next chapter examines this problem.

Summary

This chapter includes accounts of the outcome for children rescued from severe privation followed by strong intervention. If there is an absence of congenital damage, prospects are excellent. The devastating immediate effects of extremely malevolent early experiences are either greatly diminished, or so far as can be seen, entirely overcome.

CHAPTER FIVE

Outcomes of Less Severe Adversity

Signpost: *Recovery again common whenever better circumstances allow this*

This chapter follows logically from the last, testing the idea that the same forms of recovery will be apparent, though lesser in degree, as was indicated in children rescued from very severe deprivation. It will span a variety of research areas, sampling each briefly to establish whether their findings fit the main picture.

We have already referred to our own early studies (Chapter One), our search for generalization of those findings, and our immediate reward in the publication of research by Hilda Lewis (1954). Details of the latter study should now be mentioned. She reported on the progress of 500 children taken from their families, or referred by caring agencies, and placed initially in a special reception centre. They were regarded as 'the most difficult cases the county could produce'. Two hundred in the study had been removed from home on a 'fit person' order, and orders on a further 75 were later made on the centre's recommendation.

The precipitating cause of admission, often masking several other interlocking causes, included pilfering (50); uncontrollable at home or school (90); neglected (111); and loss of parental care (78). Age range was as follows: under five, 12.4 per cent (62); five to seven, 23.2 per cent (116); eight to eleven, 46 per cent (230); twelve to fifteen, 17.4 per cent (87); a further 1 per cent were over fifteen years. Thus the vast majority were above five years. The 500 children came from 363 families; 218 from 81 families came accompanied by at least one brother or sister. Thirty-two per cent came from a family of five or more children. The general background was poor, and 66 of the families were regarded as multiply deprived 'problem families'. The children had experienced many changes of school as well as of home. A quarter of all the children admitted were regarded as normal in behaviour, but normal behaviour in some cases masked poor general mental well-being. Thirty-two per cent were delinquent, 18 per cent severely neurotic, 3 per cent psychopathic, and 21 per cent normal but with slight neurotic symptoms. This was clearly a heterogeneous group of deprived children for whom some special legal measures were deemed advisable.

Lewis was able to demonstrate, in line with previous work, quite significant associations between type of background and differing types of behaviour in children. It is in the follow-up data, however, that special interest lies. She took 100 consecutive admissions (a 20% sample) between April and December 1948, omitting only 18 who were too far away to be visited. These were replaced by the next child in the list, which must overall have been reasonably representative. Two years later, detailed interviews of foster parents, or staff in children's homes or residential schools, took place, with systematic recording of home and school data, including the child's behaviour. It was surprising that, in spite of fairly severe deprivation, some 40 per cent of these children had been assessed on admission to the centre as being in 'good' (15%) or 'fair' (25%) psychological condition. Using similar criteria this increased to 75 per cent after two years, with 39 per cent in 'good' and 36 per cent in 'fair' condition. A postal inquiry, relating to 140 other children, yielded substantially the same picture. As with the Clarke and Clarke data, but at an earlier age on follow-up, there is a fading of the effects of non-repeated early experience, even though the majority of these children had suffered considerable adversity. It is also noteworthy that individual differences were quite marked in response to such adversity. No one type of placement had a monopoly of success, and none had a generally adverse effect. This is an important finding because selective factors dictated type of placement.

There are many other findings of interest in Lewis's (1954) book. As she indicates: 'If the contentions of Bender, Lowrey, Goldfarb, Bowlby and Spitz were correct, many of the Mersham children who had been separated from their mothers at an early age should not only exhibit an affectionless, psychopathic character, but should be relatively fixed in this mould ...' While children separated from their mothers at some later age were rather less satisfactory than the rest, two years after reception, the difference is not substantial. Nor did those separated for long periods or permanently before the age of two years exhibit a conspicuously worse condition. In any event, Lewis was clear that 'separation' was a symptom of a much wider range of disadvantages, including lifelong institutionalization.

In summary, Lewis's report shows, among other things, that not all children are equally affected by adverse experiences, and that, when damage does occur, a substantial fading of its effects, granted an appropriate change of environment, tends to occur over as short a period as two years.

There is no doubt that entry to hospital is an upsetting experience for young children, and that to varying extents they show disturbances of behaviour. The question is, however, whether and to what extent such disturbances persist. The studies to be reviewed differ in length of hospitalization, length of follow-up and methods of assessment. But one would expect to find at least some consistencies in the data.

Mention should be made here of Bowlby's first major revision of his 1951 views. He studied 60 children who had spent a period before the age of four in a tuberculosis sanatorium, and matched these with controls from the same school classes at late childhood follow-up. On the basis of his earlier conclusions, he had made gloomy predictions concerning probable backwardness, incapacity for friendship and maladjustment. In the event, average IQs were 107, and for the controls 110. Capacity for friendship was normal but maladjustment was present for 63 per cent, using rather broad criteria in which 42 per cent was regarded as to be normally expected. So there was a 21 per cent excess. But as the authors indicated (Bowlby *et al.* 1956), 'part of the emotional disturbance ... is to be attributed to factors other than separation' (p.213). By this they drew attention to tubercular families when illness and death were common, with attendant disturbed family relations and depressed economy. Responding to his findings, Bowlby noted that in the earlier (1951) study, the case had been 'overstated'. Later Bowlby was to defend himself for this changed view by noting that with new findings it is always the worst cases that are reported. Such extremes cannot safely be generalized, but at least they allow the identification of risk factors, and this is what he had done. There is little doubt that prolonged separation (or what we would call general deprivation), as is often found in children in care, can have very damaging effects on development (cf. Morgan 1998), especially if continued.

Schaffer (1958) studied transient disturbances in children during and following periods of hospitalization. In the latter case, those below the age of six months showed brief changes in behaviour, the 'global' syndrome. Above this age a more prolonged 'over-dependent' syndrome was observed, but, as we shall see, this faded and disappeared within a longer but reasonable time.

The better studies, such as those by Prugh *et al.* (1953) and Schaffer (1958) were concerned with short periods of hospitalization and short follow-up. In the former study a large proportion, some 68 per cent of those from a 'humanized' ward, showed significant disturbance on return home, dropping to 44 per cent after three months, and none after six months. (Controls under orthodox conditions showed even greater post-hospital disturbance, reducing to 15% after six months.) Schaffer (1958) found that 80 days marked the upper limit of disturbance for older children, and that some disturbance was typical of 72 per cent of the children. Thus both investigations concentrated upon fairly immediate effects. In contrast, a study by Douglas (1975) reported very minimal immediate post-hospital effects. In addition, his very long follow-up to adolescence yields results which he believed might reasonably be interpreted as arising from early hospitalization. This interpretation is contrary to other evidence in this book, and subsequent work offers a different explanation.

A powerful criticism was provided by Rutter *et al.* (1975a, 1975b). New data were available from two more recent epidemiological studies in the Isle of Wight and an inner London borough. Single hospital admissions lasting a week or less were again not associated with any form of later emotional or behavioural disturbance, while repeated admissions were significantly related to such problems. Multiple admissions were more likely to come from disadvantaged homes; repeated admissions may, of course, arise from chronic illness, but often represent a marker for associated adversities. Rutter *et al.*'s conclusion from this is substantially similar to our own.

In a rather different field, a similar point has been made by Wolkind, Kruk and Chaves (1976), who reported preliminary findings from a study of over 500 primiparous women. They have related early separation experiences, their type and timing, to the women's psychosocial status at the time of pregnancy. The data emerged from detailed interviews and questionnaires. A separation was recorded for any reported absence from either parent for one month before age five, and for three months after that age, unless an admission into local authority care had occurred after five, when again one month was counted as a separation. Almost 20 per cent reported separation, so defined, and these were less likely to be married, and more likely to be teenage, to have housing difficulties and a significantly higher score for pre-pregnancy malaise. The separations 'should, however, be seen not as a cause of later difficulties, but rather as a sensitive index of other experiences which might lead to these difficulties'. The authors offer evidence that it is only separation occurring within the context of a disrupted childhood which is of importance, and that it is not critical that this separation should occur at an early age. The women concerned seem to have experienced a continuity of social and family difficulties through childhood and into early adult life. It may, of course, be objected that memory for events, and particularly for their timing, is notoriously unreliable, and that to some extent it might be possible that the women's statements were inaccurate, or at least weighted by misperceptions.

Late adoption

The Skeels (1966) prospective study is a classic, originating in an accidental discovery that two infants with learning disabilities transferred from a very inadequate orphanage to a 'colony' for people with learning disabilities, and made rapid gains. As the only youngsters there, they received immense interest and stimulation from older inmates so that at age three and a half they were adopted. As a repetition of this discovery, eleven further children were transferred and nine were ultimately adopted. Twenty-five years after the last contact they were followed up and found to be very ordinary citizens, unmarked by their early austere experiences (see also Clarke and Clarke 1976, pp.214–223).

The Kadushin (1970) study of children adopted late (average age seven years), having been legally removed from adversity at an average of three and a half, followed by placement in an average of more than two foster homes, made a considerable impact on adoption practices. Followed up at an average of almost 14 years, between 82 and 87 per cent of adoptive parents expressed satisfaction about the outcome. This large group showed a greater degree of mental health and stability than might have been expected from their background and early developmental histories (cf. Lewis 1954).

A well-known adoption study by Barbara Tizard (1977) concerned children taken into care early in life and remaining in the institution for between two and seven years, until some were restored to their natural mothers and some were adopted. They were followed up at ages four and a half and eight, after a baseline assessment at age two. Data are presented on the adoptees' intellectual and social progress; at age four and a half they were doing well, with the majority of parents indicating their children's deep attachment to them. They were, however, over-friendly with strangers. An even better picture emerged at age eight, but the children's concentration was reported by teachers to be poor; they were restless and inclined to be unpopular with other children. They remained strongly attached to their parents.

A further follow-up of this group was carried out by Hodges and Tizard (1989), by which time the children had reached the age of 16. In general terms, things had gone well for 23 out of 25 adoptees; family relations for most were satisfactory, differing only a little from a carefully selected comparison group of adolescents who had never been in care. But their relationships with those outside the family, especially with peers, were less satisfactory than in the comparison group, this finding being concordant with all other adoption studies. However, Hodges (personal communication 1999), in a further follow-up of the adopted group at age 30, states that 'the evidence seems to support the view that the effects of earlier adversity fade, given the right circumstances, and the view that there are some enduring effects producing continuities in personal characteristics'. These tended to be in the area of interpersonal style of relating. Dr Hodges's full report will be of great interest.

The most striking finding lay in the difference between adopted and restored children; on all measures, intellectual, scholastic and emotional, the latter were disadvantaged compared with the adoptees. They and their parents were less often attached to each other, and where there were siblings, these were preferred to the restored child. It seems clear that the adoptive families strongly encouraged the development of attachments while those of the restored children hindered them. These children as adolescents reflected in both groups their long-term family ecological settings.

Indiscriminate friendliness with strangers by adopted children is quite commonly reported, and is a puzzling phenomenon. Chisholm (1998), in a study of Romanian adoptees, makes some useful points. Such behaviour may serve as an adaptive function in an orphanage with limited resources. These children may receive what little attention caregivers have time to give. Indiscriminate friendliness might also reflect a need for stimulation after earlier unstimulating lives. Most adults of a kindly nature are likely to reinforce such behaviour. On the question of attachments to adoptive parents, Chisholm confirms Tizard's findings and points out that the institutions from which the adoptees were drawn were far inferior to those she described (see also p.96).

A further example has been provided by Triseliotis and Russell (1984) in a retrospective study of 44 adults who had been adopted late. They had at first experienced several placements and been considered as dubious candidates for adoption because of adverse family backgrounds and emotional disturbance. The book contains a wealth of detail about their lives, including educational histories and personal and social status. The authors comment on their good adult adjustment, and their escape from the effects of severe deprivation in the context of a new, caring environment.

An article by Dumaret, Coppel-Batsch and Couraud (1997) contains a useful summary of what they regard as 'the most significant studies' of foster care outcome over the previous 30 years internationally. In their own research, they gathered information on 63 children from very disadvantaged backgrounds who had been in care from an average age of about seven years until an average of 15 and a half. They had spent at least five years with foster families and at the time of follow-up were at least 23 years of age. Data were available for 94 per cent of the sample, the majority by direct interview. Most had overcome their childhood adversities: 56 per cent were socially well integrated, 12 per cent had average integration, 20 per cent partial, with 10 per cent in situations of failure. In this cohort there had been significant evidence of past (i.e. grand-parental and parental) transmission of adversity which had largely been broken by foster care. Tribute was paid to the therapeutic and child-rearing assistance provided by the staff of the care agency. These conclusions are supported in a wide-ranging review of outcomes in long-term foster care. Longitudinal studies indicate that 'the outcome is generally much better than professional prejudice suggests' (Minty 1999).

Follow-up studies without intervention

Kolvin *et al.* (1990), in the prospective Newcastle Thousand Family Study, tracked the development of children who in early childhood had lived in deprived circumstances yet who, as adults, showed in the most part a shift into a lesser degree of problems, and included some 13 per cent who were living entirely normally. There were movements into and out of deprivation, and as the authors note, 'change is the dominant feature' (p.167). These authors believe that deprivation increases personal vulnerability, modifiable, however, by such protective factors as intelligence, equable temperament, scholastic ability and social skills.

Kolvin *et al.* pointed out that their conclusions endorse some generalizations one of us had outlined in 1978. These were that correlations consistently declined over time, and thus that individual variability was as strong as consistency. Second, personal changes always followed marked environmental changes. Third, development included substantial discontinuities as well as continuities. Fourth, averaging relationships across time can conceal important changes in a minority of individuals or sub-groups. Fifth, multiple predictive measures were likely to be more powerful than a single measure. Sixth, evidence from longitudinal studies indicated that many competent adults had severely disturbing childhoods, while many highly achieving children subsequently failed to attain their predicted potential. Seventh, behaviour has multiple determinants with a continuous interaction between person and situation; not only are people influenced by their situations, but influence them as well. Eighth, earlier narrower models which focused on the comparative effects of genetics and environment had given way to examination of the wider interaction between person and environment. Ninth, early measures, and the longer the period of prediction, the less the predictive power; such changes could not primarily be due to errors of measurement. Tenth, human development may be regarded, within limits, as potentially somewhat open-ended. These generalizations were successfully applied by Kolvin *et al.* to their longitudinal findings.

For a further analysis of the Newcastle Thousand Family Study (1947–1980), Sadowski *et al.* (1999) showed that multiple, ongoing family disadvantages in childhood substantially increased the risk of suffering a major depressive disorder in adulthood (at age 33). A background of family instability, poor mothering, poor physical care, dependence on social welfare and overcrowding were relevant associates. The baseline for this part of the study was gained from information available at age five, so here one is dealing with continuing problems based upon even earlier assessments of deprivation. Females were found to be especially vulnerable to major adult depression when they had experienced both poor mothering and poor physical care in childhood. The authors are careful to point out that in spite of these ongoing adversities, only a minority (28.2%) succumb, compared with 7.2 per cent in the general Newcastle population. Environmental experiences, of course, can fluctuate over time, some for the better and some for the worse; this fact, write the authors, may account for substantial discontinuities as well as continuities (p.117). Thus the effects of earlier life experiences can be reinforced or modified by various protective factors, both personal and social.

Sadowski *et al.*'s findings are underlined in a study by O'Connor *et al.* (1999b), who recorded the status of a large community sample of women whose parents had divorced during their childhoods. The results endorsed the well-known association between divorce and adulthood depression (and divorce), mediated by a number of ongoing influences preceding and following parental divorce, including stressful life events. As the authors indicate, 'Although parental divorce *per se* did not explain elevated depressive symptomatology in adulthood, risk factors associated with parental divorce did predict later depression' (p.788). Once again, the effects of risk can be maintained, strengthened or diminished by later circumstances.

Tonge *et al.*'s (1983) follow-up of children from multi-problem families indicated that, in adulthood, about one third lived normally, one third were marginal and another third remained seriously deprived like their parents. Ferguson, Horwood and Lynskey (1994) believe that with the passage of time young people, having left their original family environments, may be exposed to further life and socialization experiences which can override their earlier social learning. There are other important studies which indicate the individual personal role, as well as social supportive factors, in escape from early adversity.

Recovery from perinatal problems

Some of the studies already reviewed have shown strong recovery processes at work following removal to better (and often far better) circumstances. Is there evidence of such trends when children remain in relatively unchanging circumstances? Study of the outcome of perinatal difficulties has a bearing on this question, as did the previous section.

The best known longitudinal study of children who suffered perinatal damage is, perhaps, Werner's (Werner 1985, 1989; Werner and Smith 1982). She and her colleagues studied a total birth cohort of Oriental and Polynesian descent on the island of Kauai. The sample included 698 children, followed from birth until two years ten months, and in some cases until 18 and 32 years.

Neonatal and infant mortality rates were very low, but a number of infants experienced perinatal stress involving a variety of congenital disorders. 'At birth 9 per cent of the cohort had some congenital defects, of which 3.7 per cent were serious enough to require long-term, specialized care for either severe physical handicaps and/or severe mental retardation' (Werner 1985, p.337). Fourteen (or 2%) of the children surviving until two years had suffered severe perinatal stress; 69 (or 10%) had suffered moderate perinatal stress.

At each of the follow-up stages intellectual outcome was a function of a significant interaction between characteristics of the caretaking environment and degree of perinatal stress. As early as 20 months, the children growing up in middle-class homes who had experienced the most severe perinatal complications had mean scores on the Cattell Infant Scale almost comparable to those of children with *no* perinatal stress who were living in disadvantaged homes. The most developmentally retarded (in physical as well as intellectual status) were those who had both experienced perinatal stress and been reared in the poorest homes.

> The impact of the caretaking environment appeared even more powerful at age 10 years. First, children with and without severe perinatal stress who had grown up in middle-class homes both achieved mean PMA (Primary Mental Abilities) IQ scores well above the average. Second, PMA IQ scores were seriously depressed in children from low SES (socioeconomic status) homes, particularly if they had experienced severe perinatal stress. Third, the family's socioeconomic status showed significant associations with the rate of serious learning and behaviour problems. *By age 18 years, ten times as many youths with serious coping problems were living in poverty as had survived serious perinatal stress.* (Werner 1985, p.341)

The latest report (Werner 1989) focused on high-risk children, one third of whom had in adult life made satisfactory adjustments despite a combination of alcoholic or mentally disturbed parents. Many of the characteristics identifying the resilient children were already present at the age of two. Paediatricians and psychologists noted their alertness, positive social orientation and self-help skills. The author also drew attention to supportive social environmental factors that appeared to protect these young people at various points during their lifespan.

A less well known but very elegant study was presented by Wilson (1985) as an offshoot of the famous Louisville Twin Study. This important prospective longitudinal research project included 494 pairs of monozygotic and dizygotic twins and their singleton siblings, demographically representative of the metropolitan borough of Louisville, Kentucky. These twins were tested at three months, six months, twelve months, twenty-four months, three years and six years. A vast amount of personal and demographic information concerning the children and their families is available.

The cohort yielded, naturally enough, babies who were small for gestational age and also twins falling below 1750g birthweight. Would all these babies be at risk for slow development compared with the complete cohort of twins who as a group were somewhat premature, were somewhat smaller at birth and showed delayed development?

It turned out that the small-for-gestational-age infants later exhibited only a modest deficit in IQ scores (about four points) at age six, reduced from a deficit of 16 points at age three, when compared with the whole cohort. That statistical significance was greatly enhanced by the large numbers involved, outweighing their psychological importance. The author therefore concludes that small-for-gestational-age babies are at no special risk for later retardation.

The same, however, was not true of the very low birthweight babies, many of whom were also very premature. They showed a highly significant deficit at each test age throughout childhood, and although the initial deficit of 19 IQ points was eventually reduced to nine points, there was no evidence of further recovery for this group. In contrast to the small-for-gestational-age twins, most, but not all, of these infants seemed to be at a long-term disadvantage. When the group was divided by social status, although the numbers were relatively small, 17 high versus 17 low, those in the high-SES group appeared to have recovered by age six with average IQs of 101, whereas those in the low-SES group were one standard deviation below them with average IQs of 86.

> Mother's education was significantly related to recovery from 24 months onwards, which suggests that maternal intelligence plays a prominent role in determining the level of recovery. When monozygotic twins of markedly unequal birth weight were compared, the twins who weighed less than 1,750g attained the same level of IQ scores at 6 years as did their heavier co-twins. Among these genetic replicates, the initially powerful effects of low birth weight did not exert a long-term handicapping effect on mental development. The data argue for a high degree of resilience in mental development in the face of perinatal stress and for a powerful effect of heritage and home environment in guiding recovery from early deficit. (Wilson 1985, pp.69, 70)

Wilson goes on to note that developmental processes are continuous and ongoing, and possess intrinsic self-correcting tendencies. This was first identified by Waddington (1966) as one of the cardinal properties of developmental processes.

Intervention for low birthweight problems

Low birthweight (LBW) can arise from a variety of problems, whether biological or social, and from their interactions. In an important American review of the outcome of early intervention for such infants, Blair and Ramey (1997) considered eight methodologically sound recent or fairly recent studies. Reviewing causes, they point to poverty as the largest risk factor for LBW. This itself is a marker for poor access to health care and medical risks during pregnancy, as well as other environmental and behavioural adversities. The outcome for such children includes increased risks of health problems, neurodevelopmental delays and psychological deficits, compared with children of normal birthweight. In intervention studies reported in the Infant Health and Development Program (IHDP) (1990), the LBW children without intervention, as controls, were 2.7 times more likely than the intervention children to exhibit mild retardation at age three and 1.8 times more likely to suffer behaviour problems. Such children function on average in disadvantaged circumstances about half a standard deviation below their already low functioning peers, so this group operates at high risk for poor outcome (see also Wolke et al. 1995). However, as shown by Werner and Smith (1982), these difficulties can in many cases be successfully moderated by supportive factors in children's environments.

In reviewing the selected eight studies, Blair and Ramey (1997) identify factors which are relevant to success with intervention programmes. For example, intervention which was parent-focused began at birth, so to begin in the first year of life is important, engaging parents in effective caregiving routines and paying attention to individual differences. The aim is thus to help parents to become active agents of change in their child's development. The important criterion for intervention success must be the maintenance of early gains. Results at age five from the IHDP intervention are, however, not especially cheering. Only some aspects of cognitive development were affected, and there were no differences in health and behaviour between the intervention groups and controls. Of course, temperamental, motivational differences among children (and indeed parents) may impede or facilitate the intervention process. Once again, one must draw attention to transactional aspects of development and the way in which these can strongly affect the life path. There is, in this respect, an indication that maternal education and intervention effectiveness are related and, one might add, maternal IQ. Indeed, the overall conclusions from the authors' detailed review are that effectiveness reflects comprehensive early intervention, moderated by maternal education and the infant's birthweight (in turn related to lower IQ among the lower LBW infants).

Early childhood intervention programmes

From the mid-1960s onwards the field of early intervention widened and flourished, although originally 'sold' on a far too optimistic ticket, with little consideration of the importance of what followed such attempts to promote and accelerate children's development (Clarke 1968). President Johnson in the USA, as part of his War against Poverty, took advice from a number of experts on intervention, including J.S. Bruner, who chose to ignore the findings of Kirk (1958) in supporting a rapidly developed nationwide Operation Head Start. When one of us at a public meeting made critical remarks about the naïvety of an approach which suggested that cycles of deprivation could be broken by short pre-school programmes, Bruner indicated that political pressures upon the advisers had been extremely strong. The fairly rapid aftermath of Head Start was identification of the 'wash-out' pheno- menon (shown a decade earlier by Kirk) where pre-school effects faded while controls, without having experienced pre-school programmes, caught up. However, as Head Start developed, especially with Follow-Thru programmes reinforcing the early effects, matters im- proved. Nonetheless, the high hopes of a massive breakthrough for disadvantaged children were not realized. Zigler and Valentine (1979) wrote that 'in retrospect it is hard to believe that so much confidence could have been placed in one isolated year of intervention in one magic period of a child's life ... It is now my view that such tokenistic programs are worse than no programs at all. The danger ... is not so much that they damage children as that they give the appearance that something useful is being done, and thus become the substitute for more meaningful efforts' (pp. 13, 365).

During the 1970s, a self-appointed group of eminent researchers formed a Consortium for Longitudinal Studies, pooling data from a number of very special university-based programmes. Among their motives was a concern that a building bandwagon of professionals were denying the importance of early experience or continuity of experiences in later life, an idea, they felt, which denied common observations, but was based on flimsy and selective evidence (Lazar *et al.* 1977, p.5). The whole study was later presented by Lazar and Darlington (1978, 1982).

On adolescent follow-up, very significant effects of pre-school programmes on lowered special class placement, and to a less extent retention in grade, were found. Moreover, it seemed that neither type nor duration of programme, presence or absence of language goals, and training or non-training of teachers produced differential effects. As long as something good was done in the context of a high quality programme, a chain of events followed. These children were still likely to lead troubled lives, and, as Ramey (1982) put it, 'that these results obtained in spite of the efforts of some of our leading scientists and educators, testifies to the difficult and complex set of conditions associated with lower socio-economic status in this country' (p.149).

Royce, Lazar and Darlington (1983) provided a more recent report on these programmes, since a further follow-up had taken place in 1980. They indicated that steady, small programme-control differences were found throughout elementary school and junior high school and that these continued to the end of high school. Progressively higher percentages of control children failed to meet school requirements at each grade level (p.713). The oldest samples showed a 15 per cent difference for educational attainment. Those who were between 19 and 22 years of age were interviewed in detail. Those with pre-school attendance were found to have higher occupational aspirations and expectations, and expected to gain their choices. However, no differences were found in employment status, earnings, hours worked or type of job between programme and control young adults. Surprisingly, those who had been retained in grade were more likely to be employed.

In speculating about the processes involved in programme/control differences, the authors consider that the effects could be explained by an ongoing series of success exchanges or transactions, a flow of events initiated at pre-school. This is precisely what happens, for good or ill, in normal circumstances; one good or unfortunate thing usually leads to similar sequences.

Another high-quality programme, the Perry Preschool project, has from time to time been reported by Weikart's team, part of which was included in the Consortium study. Disadvantaged black children (123) were followed up in one report to age 19. They had been randomly allocated to pre-school or non-pre-school conditions at ages three or four, with the former being exposed to one- or two-year programmes by exceptionally dedicated teachers and researchers. Initial IQs lay between 60 and 90. Pre-school attendance lasted for two and a half hours per day with an additional one and a half hours per week home visit by a teacher. On follow-up, the pre-school groups differed from the non-pre-school group in the percentage of years in special education, 16 versus 28 per cent; for high school graduation, 67 versus 49 per cent; for college or vocational training, 38 versus 21 per cent; for employment, 59 versus 32 per cent; and ever detained or arrested, 16 versus 28 per cent. IQ differences had, as usual, washed out. It seems that this high-quality programme had direct, immediate effects on both parents and children, which in turn led to an ongoing transactional sequence in which effects become causes of further effects reinforced by the home, by school success, the reactions of teachers and others. However, the authors note that by itself pre-school education is no panacea (Berrueta-Clement et al. 1984).

The distinguished economist, Barnett (1996) undertook a wide-ranging and impressive assessment of benefit and costs of the Perry Preschool Program at an age 27 follow-up. There were then no differences in the modest annual male earnings between Program and No-Program males, but considerable differences between the respective female groups. There were benefits to parents of the Program children in terms of improved parenting skills and interaction with their offspring, as well as positive interaction between siblings. Specifically, the benefits to children in the Program versus No-Program groups included the following: ever classified as mentally impaired, 15 per cent versus 35 per cent; graduation from high school, 66 per cent 45 per cent; home ownership, 36 per cent versus 13 per cent; arrested by age 19, 31 per cent versus 51 per cent; 5 or more arrests through age 28, 7 per cent versus 35 per cent; received welfare through age 17, 59 per cent versus 80 per cent. Once again it is clear that ongoing, positive transactions had very significant effects, even though overlap in outcome, varying from small to moderate is evident from these figures. That is, some of the No-Program individuals on particular measures acted like the majority of the Program group, and some of the Program group scored like the majority of the No-Program individuals.

Mention must also be made of perhaps the most publicized study in the field of early intervention, the Milwaukee Project. The research began in the 1960s, when the question was raised concerning the prevalence of mild retardation in slums.

Were such cases spread randomly, or were there particular associates within the slum? Heber, Dever and Conry (1968) found that the presence of a low IQ mother was very significantly associated with mild retardation in her offspring. Specifically, mothers with IQs less than 80, comprising less than half the mothers in the Milwaukee slum, accounted for almost four-fifths of children with similarly low IQs. These findings permitted either an environmental or a genetic interpretation. Hence a very strong intervention programme, with controls, was mounted from birth to establish whether the children's development could be accelerated, preventing mild mental retardation.

The Project used a two-pronged approach, assisting black mothers and their babies in a stimulation programme over a six-year period. An error lay in assessing the Project and Control children far too frequently, leading to practice effects and grossly inflated test scores. However, differences between the two groups in such inflated scores remained large and very significant. Yet another point for intervention effects in the early years is that the structured pre-school programmes can scarcely avoid 'teaching to the test'. Young children's behavioural repertoire is limited and their pre-school experiences tend to resemble the very items upon which they are assessed. A further problem arose in that from pre-school entry at age six and onwards, intervention ceased, so that all the adversities associated with poor social conditions and poor schooling provided an antidote to the earlier intervention.

At the point of school entry the Project group's mean IQ was 120.7 with controls at 87.2. Four years after intervention had ceased the former's mean had declined to 104 and the latter's remained unchanged at 86. Educationally, too, the superiority of the Project children over controls was clear, but while this remained over the first four years of schooling, the performance of both groups fell below national norms, and as time progressed the Project children's performance first declined to the lower level of the city and then to the still lower level of inner-city schools. Moreover, the gap between the two groups decreased.

The children were again assessed at ages 12 and 14 when the Project group mean IQ was now around 100, with controls at about 90, the gap having further narrowed. The whole study has been reviewed in detail by the principal researcher, Howard Garber (1988). In his final commentary he notes that in each developmental period after infancy, 'although it is possible to maintain normal IQs, it also seems that this can be accomplished only with increasing difficulty ... it suggests most simply that there are limits to the performance benefits we can expect from an early intervention treatment ...' (p.403). This, then, is a rather pessimistic conclusion to probably one of the most ambitious pre-school programmes ever attempted, and once again raises the question of whether there can be any real efficacy unless early intervention radically alters the whole context of family and other social and school relationships. Programmes like these contrast strongly with the results of total intervention for particular individuals (as described in the previous chapter), and are, of course, enormously costly.

Another high-quality intensive scholastic intervention programme, the Abecedarian project, was reviewed by Ramey (1988). His findings, gathered from 1972 onwards, support our general thesis. Ninety children identified at birth as being at high risk for school failure and mild mental retardation had been randomly assigned in early infancy to educational intervention or control conditions (see Ramey and Campbell 1981, 1987; Ramey and Haskins 1981). At kindergarten they were again randomly assigned to school-age intervention or to control conditions. A special Home/School Resource programme was provided for school-age intervention during the first three years of elementary school, *thus continuing the early intervention*. One half of each pre-school group was so assigned. In addition, a comparison group of socially more advantaged classroom peers was selected. In terms of school achievement the results showed positive effects of early and continuing educational programmes (birth to age eight), with the children who had received early but not continuing intervention next in the hierarchy, and the high-risk controls (without any intervention) showing more evidence of school failure. Will the advantages of the intervention groups remain?

Ramey and Ramey (1992) consider this problem, offering IQ, Reading and Mathematics data up to age 12. The effect size of the early intervention is from approximately five to ten points – that is, between one-third and two-thirds of a standard deviation, highly significant. Grade failure for this group was 28 per cent, versus 55 per cent for the control children. For those with IQs less than 86, the intervention group included 13 per cent, with controls at 44 per cent. Such results, write the authors, 'support the view that *intensive* early educational intervention can produce *long-lasting* benefits, in both intellectual performance and school achievement' (p.342, authors' italics).

The authors point out that long-term evaluation of intervention benefits is complicated because of the many factors which influence the life course. We agree, and consider that where such positive influences are prolonged, the mechanism includes transactional processes across time where effects on parents and children reinforce each other. Berrueta-Clement *et al.* (1984) have suggested that immediate early effects become causes of other effects, which in turn become causes, and so on along the time continuum. Nevertheless, these processes are likely to attenuate as age increases with the common adverse social influences bearing down upon the family. It is of particular interest that early effects were quite strongly related to maternal IQ, with little deterioration up to age three in children whose mothers' IQs were above 100, unlike the children of those average or below. The steepest decline arose in those with mothers' IQ below 70. Overall, there is much in common with the other very intensive programmes such as the Milwaukee Project.

A follow-up of the Abecedarian groups at age 21 has yielded results which have much in common with the findings of the Perry Preschool Program outlined earlier. At a press conference on October 20th, 1999, Ramey indicated some of the preliminary results (Campbell and Ramey 1999). While at this age there was, of course, considerable overlap between the Program and comparison group, some important differences had nevertheless emerged: in higher education, 65 per cent of the Program group versus 40 per cent of the controls; attending a four-year college before 21, 35 per cent versus 14 per cent; had given birth by age 21, 19 per cent versus 17 per cent. IQ differences had decreased from a 17 point gap at age 3, to 5 points at age 21. Unlike the Perry Preschool Program findings, there were no differences in the amount of criminal activity between the groups. There were, however, the usual large discrepancies during the school years in terms of allocation to special education classes and repeating a grade between those who had and those who had not experienced early education.

It is worth noting that the Perry Preschool Program started when the children were much older (3 to 4 years) than those in the Abecedarian program (from birth), had much less intensive education for a shorter period of time (hours per week versus full-time) and more had the extra supplementation enjoyed by half the Abecedarian group. The authors warn that comparable results would not be obtained from mediocre or short-term programs, nor would poor quality schools sustain the benefits to children. Some authorities believe that many programs and schools can be so described.

The Head Start programmes have continued from the 1960s onwards, developing and improving, but in the main have not had the same degree of support as the high-quality university-based programmes, some of which have already been mentioned. An excellent evaluation has been provided by the US Department of Health and Human Services in an Executive Summary (1985). Seventy-two studies provided data for meta-analyses of research into Head Start's effects on cognitive development. They were virtually unanimous in showing significant gains on cognitive tests at programme termination. A gain of nine or ten IQ points on average during pre-school intervention is a common finding. Scores on tests of readiness or achievement show a similar picture. One year after programmes had ceased, IQ differences remained. Two years later, they had gone. However, the document cautiously maintains that 'children who attended Head Start are less likely to fail a grade in school or to be assigned to special education classes than children who did not attend. *However, this finding is based on very few studies*' (p.8, our italics). A further section of the Summary, based on 75 studies, considers the impact of Head Start on families. Head Start parents see benefits to their children and also to themselves; sizeable proportions participate in various paid and volunteer capacities.

Children whose parents are highly involved perform better on cognitive tests than those whose parents are less involved, although the precise reason for this correlation is unclear. Head Start's impact on child-rearing practices has produced mixed results, with some reporting positive effects and others none.

Scheerens (1987) has reported a study on compensatory education in the Netherlands. He concludes: 'Programs like these usually produce modest gains according to outcome measures made immediately after program completion, while long-term effects are even smaller, if not altogether absent' (p.110). We have provided a more detailed review elsewhere (Clarke and Clarke 1989).

In an important overview of what he terms Second Generation Research (1970–1995), Guralnick (1997) indicates that far more coherent, highly visible and well-established programmes of early intervention supports and services for children and families have emerged. 'Most agree that the early years constitute a unique opportunity for influencing child development and supporting families, an opportunity that may well maximize long-term benefits for all concerned' (p.3). We would want to add that although this is undoubtedly true, what follows the early years can reinforce or override their influence. Guralnick goes on to identify three essential family interaction patterns: (1) the quality of parent–child interaction; (2) the family's provision of diverse and appropriate experiences; and (3) the way in which the family ensures the child's health and safety. While research poses considerable problems of methodology, there is now a generally held opinion 'that early intervention programs are indeed effective, producing average effect sizes falling within the range of one half to three quarters of a standard deviation' (p.10). If this relates to immediate effects, we agree. To repeat our point, what influences follow are equally important, be they reinforcing or counteractive. Life in conditions of poverty is essentially an anti-Head Start programme.

Vulnerability and resilience

The studies reviewed so far (and others) enable us to outline some of the personal and contextual influences which promote or diminish children's life chances. Why do some succeed and others fail? Attempts will be made to answer this difficult question. Bear in mind, however, that no prospective study as yet conducted, no matter how carefully designed and or how many measures used, can give us detailed answers in individual cases. Nevertheless, there are some clues, culled from numerous studies, including those reviewed by Rutter *et al.* (1983) and Werner (1989), already discussed. Several factors seem to be protective:

1. Constitutional dispositions that will render some children attractive even to the most depraved parents and probably to other members of the family and to a wider community. These include sociability, problem-solving ability and planning ability, leading gradually to an internal locus of control. Such children are likely to attract the positive attention of teachers in school; to acquire self-esteem and self-confidence; and to believe in their own ability both to adapt to changing circumstances and to change circumstances themselves.

2. Some network of affectional support, which may be absent even in the best institutions but may be present in very disadvantaged homes.

3. Schools in which children are valued and encouraged to learn. There are by now massive research data supporting the view that schools may differentially enhance both achievement and adjustment.

4. A peer group, probably based in school, that is pro-social. This means that individual children need to be sufficiently attractive in positive ways to be chosen as friends.

5. An ability to plan purposefully, which Rutter (1989) believes will make a big difference to choice of career and/or choice of continuing education and to delaying marriage and childbearing until an appropriate time.

All these factors have been found to be protective of children at risk, in large-scale studies based in ordinary communities. In addition, there are accounts of rare intervention programmes that start in the pre-school period and either maintain their hold over certain children (as in Ramey and Campbell 1987) or initiate a sequence of positive, ongoing events, as in the well-publicized Perry Preschool Program (Berrueta-Clement *et al.* 1984; Schweinhart and Weikart 1980, 1981).

Several factors threaten positive personal development:

1. Temperamental irritability and lack of sociability, often combined with some degree of mental retardation. Infants growing up in large, chaotic, discordant families may not have the opportunity to gain an understanding of social cause and effect, nor to develop planning ability or knowledge of the desirability of delayed gratification and an internal locus of control.

2. Lack of emotional security and strong affectional ties with any one person, be it a sibling, grandmother, neighbour or other significant individual.

Children who lack these supports are likely to be rated *troublesome* by teachers and later by peers in school, to be unpopular with peers, and to seek attention and emotional support in socially undesirable ways. If they are unlucky, they will find themselves in schools that lack the necessary tranquillity and academic press to enable them to learn, returning to large, affectionless families that are unable to exercise kind but firm control. They may grow up in a social situation characterized by poverty and lack of hope, from which they lack the personal resources to escape. Problems of inner cities give rise to what Haggerty, Roughman and Pless (1975), followed by Baumeister (Baumeister and Kupstas 1990), term *the new morbidity*. This concept is not entirely new; it is the considerable increase in earlier well-known hazards that has prompted the evolution of the term. It includes behavioural and school problems among children and adolescents, environmental risks, drug and alcohol abuse, accidents, violence, adolescent pregnancy, psychiatric disorders and family disruption (Baumeister and Kupstas 1990, pp.50–51).

Summary

This chapter has intentionally been a catch-all, with brief reviews of the best studies in a variety of research areas. It is our view that the research results from these different fields are in considerable agreement. Studies of both long- and short-term separation experiences indicate that

Bowlby *et al.*'s (1956) part recantation of Bowlby's earlier views was correct; that the outcome of late adoption after early adversity is generally good; that many adults without special intervention escape their earlier apparent destiny; that, for good or ill, perinatal problems interact with the long-term caring environment; that high-quality early intervention programmes, especially if continued, and especially if they set in train ongoing positive cause–effect sequences, can benefit (within limits) disadvantaged children; and that certain personal and social factors either enhance or diminish children's life chances. All these underpin the notion that transactional influences are of considerable importance throughout the lifespan.

CHAPTER SIX

Contrary Evidence?

Signpost: *Studies of adopted Romanian orphans may suggest some modification to our thesis*

In seeking evidence which might throw doubt on our thesis, a number of common findings, sometimes thought to be relevant, can be shown either to be irrelevant or at least dubious. For example, although institutions can vary considerably, it is often indicated in general that institutional rearing is damaging to children. Usually such rearing is consequent upon early adversity, but the poor outcome for children must be ascribed both to that and to subsequent, prolonged institutional influences. In any event, outcome, good or bad, can itself be influenced by post-institutional experiences (Quinton *et al.* 1982; Rutter *et al.* 1983; see also Chapter Five).

In a useful review, Wachs and Gruen (1982), in noting what they describe as 'a highly stimulating exchange' between themselves and ourselves, go on to say that 'neither one of us convinced the other' (p.viii). Yet there seems to be little to quarrel with in their review, especially when they write: '... with certain exceptions, the vast majority of early experiences, *taken in isolation*, will not have long lasting effects unless later experiences occur which stabilize the effects of the initial experiences. These ... may occur naturally, as a result of transactions set up by the initial early experiences, or they may be built in to intervention strategies' (p.207). Wachs and Gruen have some useful things to say about early intervention and processes underlying continuities/discontinuities in development, and there is much less disagreement with aspects of our theme than these authors seem to believe. Skuse (1984) has, as noted earlier, shown that the prognosis is excellent for many very severely deprived children placed after rescue in better circumstances (see Chapter Four). But some do not do well, and this he ascribes to the presence of organic factors. It is, however, possible that without very strong intervention to overcome early developmental retardation, whether intellectual, emotional or both, a poorer progress would result. If so, such cases have not been reported.

A further point needs recognition: there is always a wide range of individual differences following intervention after adverse early experiences; some do very well, some quite well and some less well. What is it that characterizes the latter group? It may be an extreme vulnerability which later support can do rather little to minimize; or it may be that other aspects of the child's temperament (with its substantial genetic component) is also unfortunate, prompting adverse transactional feedback which in effect continues adversity. As Tizard (personal communication 1999) points out, there may also be differences in the adequacy of the intervention where, for example, new foster or adoptive parents are unresponsive or hostile. In any event, the correlated influences of biology, psychosocial environment, trans-actions and chance occurrences account for the inevitability of individual differences in outcome.

We turn now to more cogent evidence which may suggest modifications to our theme.

Attachment

Attachment studies have become more and more prevalent over the last two decades. They have their origin in Bowlby's initial interest in mother–child separation which logically developed further into research on attachment to a single figure (monotropy) which, in turn, merged into a recognition that multiple attachments normally occur. These researches gave rise to the view that the quality of early attach-ment produced internal representations, working models which would affect the nature of subsequent relationships, yet another variant of the early experience model. The family is now seen as the 'secure base' providing a reliable and readily available network of attachment relationships (Byng-Hall 1997).

Probably the most relevant and ingenious set of studies with an implication of supporting an early experience determinism have been undertaken by Fonagy, Steele and Steele (1991), Fonagy *et al.* (1994)

and Steele, Steele and Fonagy (1995); these claim an intergenerational transmission of attachment behaviour.

During first pregnancies, mothers and fathers-to-be were asked to describe their own childhood relations with their parents, and were classified as secure/insecure via the Adult Attachment Interview (AAI). After the birth of their babies the children were assessed at 12 and 18 months, enabling them to be classified as secure or insecure in the Strange Situation. Maternal perceptions of their own childhood attachment predicted subsequent infant–mother secure/insecure attachment patterns around 75 per cent of the time. Thus a high level of prediction was confirmed. Not only do the authors discuss their successful predictions, but also consider the 25 per cent 'error', examining cases where prenatally reported early attachment security coincided with insecurely attached children, as well as prenatally reported attachment insecurity related to securely attached offspring. Various speculative explanations, including some environmental circumstances, were offered. Such findings illustrate our view that a single criterion (in this case, early attachment) is unlikely to provide a wholly satisfactory account of complex behaviour, even when predictively powerful. Although Steele *et al.* (1995) discuss temperament briefly, this factor may well be of importance in the Strange Situation, especially at extremes of temperament. This characteristic, with its substantial genetic influence, may well be one of the mediating variables between parents and offspring (see also Benoit and Parker 1994; Fox, Kimmerley and Schafer 1991; Goldsmith and Alansky 1987).

Fonagy's work is particularly useful in the present context, suggesting that early attachment may have long-lasting effects, although, as we shall see, it is an open question whether early security/insecurity is a direct *causal* influence on adult outcome, or whether it is a marker for ongoing influences throughout childhood and adolescence. After all, the parents-to-be were asked to reflect on their whole childhoods, not just the very earliest years, of which memories would be fragmentary. If temperament is, indeed, one of several mediators, its ongoing continuity in some cases may reflect indirectly from early attachment. In a notable review, Rutter (1995) believes that 'we are very far from having reached an understanding of the development of relationships or of the ways in which distortions in relationships play a role in psychopathology ... attachment is not the whole of relationships' (p.566).

Commenting on Fonagy's work, Holmes (1998) refers to the Adult Attachment Interview, believing that the way people talk about themselves manifests an inner representation of self–other relationships, and that these derive from early parent–child interaction. 'Narrative patterns are thus both an effect of parental handling in childhood and a cause of future patterns of relationship with intimates' (p.279). Earlier, Holmes (1993) had commented upon the Adult Attachment Interview as 'revealing feelings about current and past attachments and separations, and [tapping] into emotional responses to loss difficulty. Interviews are rated not so much for their content as for the way in which the subject describes their [sic] lives and losses' (p.433). As outlined, this technique does not only reveal early responses, but also later ones. In any event, the Adult Attachment Interview presumably cannot possibly capture the origins of individual attachment, only the later relations which, of course, may, or perhaps may not, directly follow from the earlier situation.

Kagan (1998) offers several examples of problems in the interpretation of the Strange Situation in measuring early attachment. For example, attachment classifications are not very stable over periods as short as six months, although a number of studies claim greater stability (see review by Melhuish 1993). Is it likely, he asks, that any 20-minute observation can uncover psychological products created over 6000 hours of parent–child interaction? More important, 15 to 20 per cent of children are genetically programmed to become fearful in novel situations, including therefore the Strange Situation. Labelled insecurely attached, many will have had sensitive, predictable mothers. Or again, infants who have experienced day centres are used to separation, and are less likely to cry when the mother leaves. They continue to play when the mother returns, but they, too, are labelled insecurely attached. Kagan offers many more research findings which lead him to question the view that the Strange Situation can capture accurately the infant's emotional relationships over the previous 12 months. He questions, too, the interpretations usually offered about the Adult Attachment Interview. This method implies a belief that the infant's attachment quality is transformed into a 'Working Model' of future relationships, detectable in adults when they reminisce about their childhoods. In turn, this may affect the way in which parents respond to their own child. Few psychologists would believe that an adult's conception of friendship derives from his or her early experiences of a day care centre, nor would they think that early speech had profound effects on adult linguistic competence. And few have questioned whether the mother's verbal sophistication, temperament and ease or tension with an unfamiliar interviewer might influence the form of her narrative (Kagan 1998).

Kohnstamm and Mervielde (1998) ask:

> What is cause and what is effect? Is the attachment relation with the child really influenced by the parents' thoughts about their own past, as most researchers in this area seem to think, or is the present quality of the relation with the child actually influencing the parents' memories? Or are both true? As long as this is unclear it would perhaps be better to use the phrase *intergenerational concordance* or *congruence* instead of *intergenerational transmission* of the quality of attachment relations. The latter phrase suggests a one-way causal pathway only. (p.433)

One awaits with interest further work in this area. Summarizing so far, to some of the objections to the above one-way (and powerful) causality, one notes that (1) most outcomes are influenced by multiple, interacting factors, not just by one; (2) the Adult Attachment Interview assesses memories of the whole of childhood, not merely the very early years; (3) temperamental differences are likely to be one of the many mediating factors between memories of early attachments and later parental behaviour as assessed intergenerationally via the Strange Situation; and (4) the direction of causality, if indeed causality is involved, is unclear.

Sroufe, Egeland and Kreuzer (1990) have reported part of an ambitious prospective longitudinal study of children drawn from lower socio-economic groups. They used a range of measures, including assessments of the home environment, quality of attachment at 12 and 18 months (in the Strange Situation); tool problem assessment (graded problems with mother's assistance) at 24 months; teaching tasks with mother's direction at 42 months; curiosity box (child's readiness to explore) at 54 months; teacher rankings and behaviour problems (at kindergarten); home evaluation (30 months and 6 years); and counsellor ratings (age 10). One small group (N=11) out of a large set showed consistent positive adaptation from 12 to 24 months, then showed poor adaptation during the 42- to 54-month period. However, these children showed the greatest capacity for later rebound in the elementary school years, despite poor functioning in the pre-school period.

The issues are complex, write the authors, but one possibility is that the impact of early experience may remain dormant in certain contexts, only to be expressed later, as shown in some research using animals. We anticipated this general view (1968) in suggesting a possibility that the effects of early experience might be overcome but under stress might be reactivated. However, much later we examined critically the concept of 'sleeper effects', raising doubts whether this was a useful model (Clarke and Clarke 1981, 1982). Overall, Sroufe *et al.* believe that the results indicate that adaptation is always a product of both developmental history and current circumstances. In so far as this is a study of children who did not experience major life changes, the finding that early adaptation plays some part in later functioning is by no means inconsistent with our theme. See also Carlson and Sroufe (1995), however, who now believe that attachment organization provides the basis for personality functioning.

Belsky *et al.* (1996) have reported on two very much larger samples in an effort to assess the stability of early infant–parent attachment security. They recall that 'according to attachment theory, the infant during the second half of the first year of life develops an internal representation of the attachment relationship. Once found this representation is relatively stable (although still subject to modification based on subsequent experience) and guides the infant's behaviour in new situations' (p.921). Both samples were assessed at 12 and 18 months, and one further evaluation included infant–father attachment at 13 and 20 months. Rates of stability were no more than would be expected by chance, averaging about 50 per cent. The authors indicate, critically, that nearly a decade had passed since data on stability has appeared, that samples were modest in size, that corrections for chance associations had not been made and that much had changed in the way that Strange Situations are scored, and that there have also been changes in the ecology of infancy. This study underlines the complexity of the whole field of attachment classification. The question about chance associations is a very important one. For example, between two-thirds and three-quarters of non-risk samples can be expected to have participants classified as secure. By randomly assigning secure classifications to this percentage of members at two times of assessment, a high level of concordance will be achieved, inflating the appearance of stability (p.923). For a further overview, see Melhuish (1993).

Summing up, in view of the poor predictive quality of other early life characteristics, it seems unlikely that early attachment is an exception, on its own, in predicting the quality of later relationships. But the nature of early attachment can, of course, set in train ongoing consequences if there are environmental continuities.

Romanian adoptees

In the area with which this book is concerned the most important research of the decade has been carried out by Rutter and the English and Romanian Adoptees (ERA) Study Team (1998, 1999b); these articles are very detailed and complex. Selected from a larger group on carefully described criteria, 111 Romanian orphans who had been brought to England before the age of two years were followed up to age four. They had all been victims of severe global privation and on arrival had entered adoptive homes. At the same time, 52 within-country UK adoptees, placed before six months, formed a comparison group, again studied at age four and later by O'Connor *et al.* (1999a) at age six.

Romanian records on the children were rather skimpy, but in most cases yielded information on height, weight and head circumference. Within the UK, apart from physical measures, reliance for the initial assessment was placed on adoptive parents' retrospective reporting, from which Denver developmental quotients were derived. The children proved to be severely developmentally impaired and severely malnourished on arrival, with almost half below the 3rd percentile on height, weight, head circumference and IQ, this latter giving a mean of 63 (i.e. mild retardation, but with a wide range). Many suffered recurrent intestinal and respiratory infections. Here it should be noted that children placed before the age of six months were of initially higher status than the remainder of the cohort. This will be discussed later.

The authors offer a brief picture of conditions in the Romanian orphanages. These varied from 'poor' to 'appalling'. The infants were in most cases confined to cots, there were few if any playthings, little talk from 'carers', and no personalized caregiving. They were fed with gruel from propped-up bottles with large teats. Washing often involved the child being hosed down with cold water. Half the group had been institutionalized for the whole of their lives, the remainder having spent varying periods within families or at least half their lives in an institution.

From time to time (e.g. Clarke and Clarke 1976) we have indicated that across a wide age range for adoptive placement, the older members of all adoptive samples always, on average, do less well than the younger. We have attributed this to selective factors in the later adoptions. In the present study, the authors point out that selective factors on age of adoption (between six months, or above that figure) are very unlikely to have occurred. Hence any differences to be found at the age four follow-up must have arisen from differing pre-adoption experiences. This is undoubtedly correct. For us, the main finding (among several interesting subsidiary ones) is the initial average difference on the Denver Scale between the earlier (before six months) and later adopted (76.5 and 48.1, a difference of 28.4 points).

By age four, an immense catch-up had taken place, as measured on the McCarthy Scale. The mean for the whole group had risen by 36.2 points, being by now 99.2 (with a large standard deviation of 19.2 points). The within-UK comparison group, by contrast, now had a mean of 109.4 (with a smaller SD of 14.8). Physically, too, there had been great improvements. Whereas originally 51 per cent of the Romanian adoptees were below the 3rd percentile for weight, only 2 per cent were so impaired at age four.

Both the Denver and McCarthy scales showed that children adopted before the age of six months (N=56) were closely comparable to the development of the within-UK sample, in spite of the severe physical and developmental retardation on entry to the UK. Their mean scores (age four) lay between 106 and 116, depending on the scale used – that is, spanning the average of the within-UK adoptees.

The mean scores of those adopted between 6 and 24 months were, however, at age 4 below 100 (92 and 97, respectively), so they were very significantly lower than the before age 6 months and the within-UK adoptees. These later adopted children were, on average, within the normal range, although about a standard deviation below the early adopted children. Their relatively depressed scores were related partly to the presence of seven intellectually impaired children not found in the within-UK sample, and partly to an overall smaller catch-up of their group. The authors' general inference is that the deficit probably reflects the influence of some aspects of institutional rearing. They also indicate from physical data that the differential catch-up did not simply reflect the level of malnutrition which was therefore not a major determinant of cognitive outcome.

A number of qualifications were pointed out. For example, in almost all cases, psychological privation was accompanied by malnutrition. Thus, it could be that the effects of such privation are increased by the co-occurrence of malnutrition, a multiplicative effect.

In summarizing some aspects of this important study we note:

1. On average, by age four the Romanian adoptees had made dramatic gains, both physically and cognitively.

2. Their average status at four years was nevertheless significantly below the average of the controls, the within-UK adoptees. This is perhaps unsurprising because it seems possible that the parents of such children, in the very adverse conditions in Romania, would themselves be below average. Less able parents would presumably be more likely to abandon their children than more gifted families.

3. Although the initial developmental quotients of the Romanian adoptees came from baseline adoptive parent reports which were perhaps less reliable accounts than the physical measures, both sets of data were reasonably confirmatory of each other.

4. For us, a major finding lay in the differences between those aged below six months on entry to the UK, and those who were older. These differences were apparent both initially and again at age four. Part of this relative deficit reflected the presence of seven severely intellectually impaired children.

5. Those adopted before six months, as well as those adopted later, made massive gains on average, but the smaller gains in the later adopted group (from a lower baseline) must have arisen from the longer period of privation. This suggests a sensitive (but not critical) period in children who experienced privation, both physically and psychologically. It is of interest that, overall, adoptive breakdown was only 1.8 per cent, below that of within-UK adoptees, so it seems that emotional damage which usually leads to breakdown had in most been sufficiently repaired to allow adoption to proceed without insuperable problems.

A further and even more recent report has come from Rutter *et al.* (1999b). Pointing out that in earlier studies of deprived, institution-reared children there have been no comments on the occurrence of autism, and that the same applies (with just two exceptions) to case studies, the senior author became aware of autistic-like development in some of the Romanian adoptees. The total sample includes the 111 already referred to, and a further group of older children not discussed here. Qualitative analyses have focused on the 111, for whom data were available both at age four and six. There was also a contrast group of 28 'ordinary' autistic children, as well as a further group of 52 UK-adopted children placed before six months.

Autistic-like features were most marked at age four but tended to diminish greatly over the next two years. Eleven children were identified, showing difficulties in social relationships and in communication (e.g. problems in social reciprocity, eye-to-eye gaze, impaired language development). In most, too, there were preoccupations with sensations and intense, narrow interests; these came to a peak well after arrival in the UK. The behavioural patterns of these 11 were not identical. One child who arrived before the age of six months progressed well, lost language at about 20 months, became socially unresponsive, but within the next year language returned, normal social behaviour was regained and at school age he appeared completely normal. He was then excluded from further comment. The remaining ten divided into three children whose autistic features were associated with severe learning disablement and seven whose general cognitive score exceeded 50 (average score 57). Of these, six children had been assessed at both four and six years, and thus formed the basis of the analysis which is of particular interest.

The first three (learning disabled children) came late to the UK (between ages 21 and 34 months), all having experienced extremely poor institutional rearing, one being exceptionally severely malnourished. All three had something unusual in their histories, one being very premature at birth (weighing 2 lbs); another had a high-tone hearing loss and came from an orphanage with a record of high infant mortality; and the last had been isolated in a single room because of racial discrimination and illegal status. Two had a head circumference below the 3rd percentile at age six. While these three showed behaviour close to classic autism, nevertheless all had learned Makaton sign language, two made considerable social approaches, though deviant in quality, and one had improved greatly, halving his autistic score in two years. So there were quite a number of features uncharacteristic of autism.

Turning to the sub-group of six children without severe cognitive impairment, but with quasi-autistic behaviour, how did they differ from the contrast group of 'ordinary' autistic children? First, at four years there were no apparent differences. Second, by age six the situation was quite different in that the diagnostic scores were by then significantly lower (i.e. better) than in the contrast group. So, third, the improvements over a comparatively short time were atypical. The contrast children had become worse, while the Romanian quasi-autistic orphans had improved, including a tendency for IQ increment averaging 20 points. Even so, they still averaged 32 points below the rest of the sample at age six. Note that early in their development there had been nothing especially different from the also unusual behaviour of the other adoptees. The quasi-autistic behaviour, as indicated above, had developed between arrival and four years of age.

In discussing the causes of quasi-autistic behaviour, the authors offer three possibilities. First, there might have been some deviant development of attachment relationships, also noted by Chisholm *et al.* (1995) and Chisholm (1998). Second, the greater degree of cognitive impairment in these children, compared with their non-quasi-autistic peers, perhaps reflected an extreme lack of active experiences, social and non-social, resulting from prolonged confinement to cots, lack of toys and of linguistic exchanges with adults. Third, as with blind children who have a higher than usual incidence of autistic behaviour, especially if also retarded, perhaps their isolation played a comparable role. But it is important to remember that the great majority of adoptees did not respond in this way; only some six per cent did.

As noted earlier, across a wide age range at which adoption takes place, older adoptees tend to do less well than younger ones. In the case of Rutter and Chisholm studies, selective factors which may have been relevant in other studies do not appear probable. Tizard (personal communication 1999) suspects that the nature of the earlier deprivation or privation, and the characteristics of the new environment, are important in outcome. Abuse and cruelty may have different effects than institutional neglect, and many parents who adopt older children are totally ill-prepared for, and horrified by, the problems they meet. Transactional effects then follow.

A further follow-up of the whole age four cohort of Romanian orphans took place at age six, and the report awaits publication (O'Connor and the ERA Team 1999a). The senior author has kindly provided a preprint. To recapitulate, 111 Romanian orphanage children, suffering from global severe privation, were adopted in the UK before the age of two years. On the whole, after two years in adoptive homes (at age four) they had shown, on average, dramatic improvement, and many continued to gain cognitively until the second psychometric test at six years. Within this large cohort there were, of course, differences in outcome. Children adopted after six months (59 altogether) included seven who at the age of four were found to be seriously mentally retarded, but even making allowances for these children, these differences remained at age six, so that the gap between the pre- and post-six-month-old adoptees was maintained rather than closed. Even so, within the later (7–24 months) children there were 28 out of 59 who scored 100 or above, of whom seven gained 120 or more.

A number of even later adopted children admitted after the age of two years had been too old to be tested at the first follow-up (at age four), but were available at age six. These late-placed adoptees included 26 adopted between 24 and 30 months, 16 between 31 and 36 months and six between 37 and 42 months. Thus by the age six follow-up, there were available the adoptees first assessed at age four, plus a further 48 adopted after age two. The large differences in length of severe privation enable one to estimate its effects upon recovery from the impaired level at arrival.

An important investigation of sub-samples of the whole age six cohort is recorded in an Appendix. In this study, children admitted to the UK between 0 and 18 months were compared with those adopted very late, after 24 to 42 months in the institution. These two samples had each experienced roughly two and a half to four years in adoption – that is, duration of adoption was the same. For the purposes of the study it had been held constant, the main difference being the time spent in severely deprived circumstances. A very large average cognitive difference was recorded in favour of the earlier (to repeat, 0–18 months) adopted group, even though a number of these children would have passed the six-month sensitive period.

The article includes a scattergram showing the relation between the children's ages at entry to the adoptive home, against their age six general ability scores. Taking age eight months or later adoption (that is, well clear of the six months watershed), 11 children scored 120 or above, with four of 130 or above, very superior ability. Against this, some 25 children scored below 85, the arbitrary borderline for well below average ability. Among these were the seven referred to earlier who were probably constitutionally learning disabled. The majority of the eight months or later adopted sub-sample scored between 85 and 119. We see, then, very large differences in age six cognitive outcome, and that late and sometimes very late (e.g. age three and a half) adoption neither precludes superior ability, nor significantly below average functioning. Hence factors other than prolonged, severe privation must be involved. What these might be is a matter for speculation, but one obvious candidate is the genetic differences between individuals.

The authors conclude that duration of severe global privation was the more powerful predictor of individual differences in outcome than was the time spent in the adoptive home, beyond approximately the two years in which recovery took place. In view of these dramatic gains, it cannot be concluded that there is a critical period for cognitive ability around six months, but one must keep open the possibility that for many there may be a sensitive period around this time, as many writers have suggested. In view of the number of later adopted children who were of average to superior ability at age six, it is clear that the sensitive period failed to have universal effects.

Chisholm *et al.* (1995) and Chisholm (1998) have reported a study with similar implications to those of Rutter *et al.* Measuring security/insecurity of attachment and indiscriminate friendliness to previously unknown adults, their sample of adopted Romanian orphanage children showed differences between those adopted before eight months and others adopted between eight months and 68 months (median length of time in an orphanage, 17.5 months). Security of attachment was assessed in the child's own home; some 35 per cent of the early adoptees versus 58 per cent of later adopted showed insecure patterns of behaviour. However, on parent report, the early adopted did not differ from later adopted, nor from controls, on this type of behaviour. Parent report nevertheless indicated that the later adopted showed more indiscriminately friendly behaviour than the early adopted. So there is a degree of similarity between Rutter *et al.*'s cognitive studies and the attachment research of Chisholm.

These ongoing studies have been considered at length because they may suggest some modification to our theme. It has, of course, been known for many years that around six to seven months of age there comes a profound psychological change (e.g. the sudden 'fear of strangers' and 'six-month anxiety'). This was shown empirically in Schaffer's (1958) study of the later effects of hospitalization in infants. Below the age of six months, the children showed brief 'global' disturbance on returning home. Above this age, the older children were 'over-dependent' on their mothers for a much longer time.

In a different research area a study of full-term singletons by Skuse *et al.* (1994) included a group of children with serious growth faltering in their first year of life. The authors point out several possible influences, ranging from under-nutrition, congenital factors, child characteristics and inadequate parenting, as well as interactions between some of these. For example, the authors suggest that poor nutrition early in life may make a child more vulnerable to low levels of stimulation. The main general conclusion of this study is that growth faltering in the first six months of life is associated with poorer mental and psychomotor development measured in the second year. This, then, is additional evidence for a sensitive period in the first year of life. However, it is probable that such children almost certainly experienced continuities in whatever aspects of child rearing which may be assumed to have played some part in growth faltering. It is well known that the brain in the third trimester of pregnancy and the first year of post-natal life is especially vulnerable during its major growth spurt. One notes that growth deceleration in those where it first appeared after the age of six months showed no difference from a comparison group in the assessment measures used.

In spite of the above suggestion of a sensitive period, many of the studies quoted in this book relate to the outcome for older (and sometimes much older) children whose lives had altered radically for the better. These, too, exhibited considerable catch-up. Even so, their outcome might have been even better had the life changes occurred early. However, considering such studies as those by Koluchová (1972, 1976, 1991) where the privation, both physically and psychologically, was surely at least as great as that suffered by the Romanian adoptees, it seemed that total recovery had taken place (see Chapter Four). In this study, however, the children's first year was spent in care, followed by six months with an aunt, after which five and a half years of gross privation took place. But the twins were together (see pp.51–52). So there remains a puzzle, and further follow-up of the Romanian group may – or may not – show a closing gap between the early and later adopted children.

Summary

Among the several research areas reviewed in this chapter, only studies of adopted Romanian orphans may suggest modification to our thesis. Following conditions of severe global privation, those babies rescued before the age of six months made, on average, spectacular gains in development by age four, maintained at age six. The children adopted after the age of six months also made massive average gains, though not as great, from an initially lower level, even though they included seven who were functioning as almost certainly permanently learning disabled. But the difference between before and after six months must have reflected lengthier institutional privation, suggesting a sensitive (but not critical) period in their lives. But this sensitive period was not universal; some children did well or very well cognitively, even though adopted after (and sometimes long after) six months, both at age four and six follow-up. Genetic differences could be one of several possible factors explaining these outcomes. Results with similar indications were reported by Chisholm. Will these differences be maintained, or will the gap close as the children age, as has apparently happened in other cases? (See Chapter Four) There is, however, a paradox in that many other studies show immense resilience in children rescued from very prolonged adversity at sometimes much later ages.

CHAPTER SEVEN

Epilogue

Signpost: *An overview*

In this book we have traced the genesis of an idea, originating in our own early work, that contrary to received wisdom dating from Plato onwards, early experience represents no more than a first (and important) step on a long and complex path through life. Such experience does not *by itself* set for the child a predetermined future. Indeed, *by itself* its long-term influence may be negligible. When reinforced, however, its effects will be strengthened.

Of course, most children receive, as they develop, at least some degree of continuity in the sort of care they receive in their earliest years, whether good, bad or indifferent. In these cases, for the vast majority, some correlation between early and later is to be expected. Follow-up studies of such children show this, although quite often there is for some individuals a break away from what would have been a reasonable prediction. Take the Terman study, for example (pp.36–37), in which a sizeable minority of very gifted children turned out much less well than expected (Oden 1968). This should not surprise us if the major, ongoing life influences are recalled. First, the biological trajectories for different processes are not static but develop, with switching on and switching off, throughout the lifespan. Second, the psychosocial trajectory is equally likely to involve major differences at different ages, especially at life transitions. Third, transactional processes can operate powerfully, especially at extremes of temperament or intelligence. Last, and by no means least, fortuitous events or encounters can enhance or diminish life prospects. Although these four reciprocal influences will tend to co-vary, an alteration in one may well affect the others and thus the whole life path.

In spite of the problem of comparing like with like at different ages, it was noted (Chapter Three) that for normal development, researchers have failed to demonstrate anything other than weak continuities between early measures and adult status. This in itself argues against a predeterministic role for early characteristics.

Turning to the studies which tracked the development of children who had undergone major life changes, we noted that although differences in response between individuals were usually present, the average move was always in the direction of the life change. Studies of those rescued from extreme privation, as well as from less severe adversity, underlined the resilience of many (pp.49–58). We need to know more about the outcome for children whose situation seriously deteriorates; these are usually unreported.

Some of the internal, personal characteristics which assist children's adaptation or maladaptation have been noted, as well as the external supportive or disruptive factors which interact with the individual. Some children are crushed by what others experience as minimal stressors, others overcome what seem to be almost insuperable malevolent influences. Differences in vulnerability and resilience are large (pp.80–81).

Three criteria describe the essence of scientific method. First, is the study and its results repeatable by others; second, are there alternative explanations for the findings; and third, are the hypotheses to account for the findings falsifiable? The references available in this book enable hundreds of studies to be identified. Depending on the sample, the length of the follow-up, the measures used, the strength of subsequent influences and life occurrences after the early years, then loud and clear comes the message that early experience by itself does not predestine the life path, except in very rare instances where biological damage is so great as to disable the child permanently. Such gross damage results in severe learning difficulties, but there could be more subtle influences when, for example, privation, with malnutrition, might possibly handicap brain development (cf. Greenough, Black and Wallace 1987).

So the first two criteria are satisfied. But is the thesis falsifiable? It would be so if it could be shown that neurologically intact children moved from adversity to something better, yet remained equally damaged and totally unresponsive to the change. *We know of no such study.* However, might our thesis need to be modified as opposed to falsified? One well-controlled study by Rutter *et al.* (1998), supplemented by others, could be in this category (see pp.89–96). To recapitulate, a large cohort of Romanian orphanage children, removed to UK-adoptive upbringing before the age of two years, on average, at age four showed dramatic improvement, but within their cohort there occurred differential cognitive recovery in that those adopted before the age of six months did, on average, better than those adopted after six months. But the post-six-month-old adoptees did show considerable average improvement, even though seven were significantly and probably permanently retarded. For the vast majority the effects of privation had to a lesser extent faded. O'Connor *et al.* (1999a) conclude that duration of severe privation was the more important predictor of outcome than the time spent in the adoptive home beyond a two-year recovery period. In view of the dramatic average improvement, we cannot speak of a critical period for cognitive ability in early infancy. But one should keep open the possibility that *for some* there is a sensitive period around six months when further privation is associated with less, and in some cases far less, spectacular gains. But this sensitive period, as implied, failed to have universal effects; for example, of 59 children placed between 7 and 24 months, 28 scored 100 or above, of whom seven gained 120 or more. And of another 48 children placed very late (between two and three and a half years), 15 scored 100 or above, of whom six gained 120 or more. So factors other than privation must be involved. One notes that very late recovery from early deprivation can occur in the teens and early adult life (Clarke *et al.* 1958). Chisholm (1998) and Chisholm *et al.* (1995) (pp.93–94; 96) used non-cognitive characteristics (that is, attachment security/insecurity and indiscriminate friendliness with unknown adults as measures), and the implication of the findings are similar to those of the ERA Team.

So what are our overall conclusions? Recognition that, as we have repeatedly indicated in the past, the life path is *potentially somewhat* open-ended is of very great practical and theoretical significance. The two italicized words are important. Many individuals have the potential for a better life path, yet are so locked into an unfortunate personal and environmental track that they cannot escape. Whether emotionally or intellectually, they under-function. And the word 'somewhat' is equally significant. Each of us has 'ceilings' in development laid down in our DNA above which we cannot journey, and below which adversity can plunge us.

We are not the only ones (Clarke and Clarke 1992; Kagan 1998) to have advanced the view that there is a degree of developmental uncertainty in predicting the life path. Indeed, this was implicit in some of the very early work tracing the growth of single characteristics such as intelligence or scholastic attainment. Rutter (1989) points out that 'chain' effects during development are common. 'Life transitions have to be considered both as end products of past processes and as instigators of future ones ... as both independent and dependent variables' (p.46). We, too, suggested (1992, p.154) that development involves a series of linkages in which characteristics in each period have a probability of linking with those in another period. But probabilities are not certainties, and deflections of the life path, for good or ill, are possible, although always within the powerful limits imposed by genetic, constitutional and social trajectories. Good or bad 'luck' can also play a crucial role. Schaffer (1992) notes: 'The idea that specific experiences, occurring at specific points of time ... can in themselves have long-term consequences must be reflected in favour of a much more complicated, multi-determined and continuing process' (p.51).

A few years before he died, the ever courageous Bowlby took account of the researches which we have sampled here. He wrote:

> ... the central task ... is to study the endless interactions of internal and external [factors], and how the one is influencing the other not only during childhood but during adolescence and adult life as well ... Present knowledge requires that a theory of developmental pathways should replace theories that involve specific phases of development in which it is postulated that a person may become fixated and/or to which he may regress. (1988, pp.1–2)

However, in the teeth of the evidence we have provided, there is still resistance to accepting our thesis. For example, in the quality press one notes reports of disturbed individuals whose problems are ascribed only to the early years, often ignoring the adversities which continued. Professionals, too, both initiate and maintain such views. Kagan (1992, p.993) reflects upon this in writing:

... the indefinite preservation of a young child's salient qualities, whether intellectual ability or a secure attachment, remains an ascendant assumption in developmental work ... There is an inconsistency between the contemporary commitment to the importance of the local context which changes, and a belief in the capacity of early encounters to create immutable structures which will be preserved. (see also Kagan 1998)

Rutter (1999) indicates that the 'chain effects' across time, referred to earlier, are mainly indirect rather than direct from early experience. The probable mechanisms might involve changes in the way the individual processes the experiences, or effects on the neuro-endocrine system, or vicious cycles of maladaptation (p.485).

In an important review article, Schaffer (2000) reiterates that the search for the effects of early experiences needs to be a much more complex enterprise than was at first realized. One must take account of the ever greater number of factors known to be relevant over and above early experience itself. Subsequent influences can modulate the earlier effects; we know that early experience does not have a dominant role on its own and that reversal may be feasible.

It seems probable that a very large proportion of the world's population is under-functioning, whether intellectually, educationally or emotionally. We know from the studies we have outlined that much could be done to diminish this tragic waste of human potential. But we recognize also that societies lack the will and the resources, both human and financial, to make any great impact on the problem. However, the knowledge provided by these many researchers at least helps us to understand that the life path is not predetermined by the experiences of the early years alone, but results from the long-term cumulative development of genetic and environmental interactions and transactions. This knowledge should begin to inform social policies. For example, of 34,000 children in continuous care in this country in 1995, almost half had been abused or neglected or considered to be at risk of abuse or neglect (Morgan 1998). Growing up in care is likely to reinforce early damage and make it likely that these children, without *strong* intervention via fostering or adoption (in spite of the difficulties), will continue their probably doomed life path. The human and social costs of failure in tackling this problem are immeasurable. The huge costs of remediation will need to be balanced by the huge long-term costs of inaction. Society too often favours the latter.

It is now reported by House of Commons researchers that some local authorities are reluctant to promote adoption of children in care. For example, in the ten 'worst' authorities looking after a total of 3814 children in 1997 there were only 32 adoptions (*The Independent*, 7 April 1999). Need one comment further? Tizard (personal communication 1999) believes that the major social work error is to delay the adoption decision, supporting the natural parents in the hope that matters will improve, until eventually the children are so damaged that they become 'hard to place'.

It is also alleged that some social workers subscribe to an 'anti-adoption culture' partly because of the undoubted difficulties in dealing with damaged children, and partly in seeking impossibly high standards in finding a 'perfect match' between child and adoptive parents. Tizard also suggests that the underlying factor is their objection to adoption as such because of the supposed damage for the child's identity, and to the emotional balance of the natural mother. Of course, many of these children are in care temporarily, to be returned in due course to the circumstances probably resembling those which originally gave rise to these placements. Again, need one comment?

It is also said that one child in three is born to a family 'living in poverty' (i.e. with less than half the average national income after housing costs are taken into account). The number of children living in such households has tripled in the last 20 years to four million. Recently (April 1999), the Government has pledged to wipe out child poverty within 20 years. Such a programme would demand attention to a spectrum of social concomitants, including what some Americans term the 'new morbidity' (Baumeister and Kupstas 1990). There has been a considerable increase in earlier known hazards such as behavioural and school problems, drug and alcohol abuse, accidents, violence, adolescent pregnancy, family disruption and neighbourhood breakdown. These pose problems of almost overwhelming complexity, yet some of the research findings outlined in this book have clear implications for part of the social restitutive process.

Summarizing this overview chapter we conclude that

1. theories ascribing overwhelming, disproportionate and predeterministic importances to the early years are clearly erroneous;

2. the widespread belief in the disproportionate effects of early experiences is likely to lead to underestimation of what can be done for deprived children, and hence, on the one hand, less than adequate interventions, or, on the other, total inaction;

3. there is no suggestion that what happens in the early years is unimportant. For most children, however, the effects of such experiences represent no more than a first step in an ongoing life path which may be straight or winding, incremental or decremental, depending on the two-way relationship between individuals and their contexts. There is little indication that any one point of development is more critical than another; all are important. And in the ongoing shaping or reshaping of the person's life path, it is to continuing influences that significance must be ascribed.

Frequently Asked Questions

Sometimes students ask us searching, if sometimes rather muddled, questions about our thesis; here is a sample of them:

Q. From what you say, early experience doesn't matter, since adverse effects can be made good; is this your argument?

A. No, early experience does matter. First, for humane reasons one deplores adverse early experiences and suffering. Second, the quality of the first steps on the life path is usually followed by similar influences, whether good, bad or indifferent. So for most children early experiences are continued, but they need not be. The cycle can be broken at any point, certainly up to young adulthood.

Q. You seem to be environmentalists, is this so?

A. Certainly not! We have always stressed the interactions between genes and environment. Remember that the former do not dictate an exact outcome, but rather provide a framework of possibilities. Such interactions and, perhaps especially, transactions determine where in this range the particular outcome can occur. In any event, the holding of extreme environmentalist or hereditarian views is totally unwarranted in the light of modern research.

Q. You've talked about the life path being 'potentially somewhat open-ended'. Doesn't age exercise increasing constraints upon change?

A. We suspect so, especially where gross privation has occurred. Discovery of such cases, because of the child's increasing physical size, has normally occurred no later than middle childhood

(Genie was an exception – see p.50). It is possible that longer periods of privation would produce unalterable change. When lesser degrees of deprivation have been identified, changes for the better – that is, recovery have been recorded up to and including early adulthood. Later than this, most people, for personal and social reasons, tend to get locked into a predictable life path. Exceptions include late psychiatric problems.

Q. Are some stages in development more important than others?

A. So far as we can judge, the whole of development is important, although the first 30 years of life usually (but not always!) begin to stabilize the life path. However, it is at major life transitions (e.g. school entry, adolescence, marriage or divorce, bereavement, retirement) that the individual is likely to be under stress and sometimes the path takes a new turning. Hence to understand the nature of development one needs to study the whole lifespan.

Q. What factors influence childhood resilience?

A. These have been outlined earlier (pp.80–81). They involve both personal characteristics and their interactions with the degree of support provided in the social environment. Obviously the stronger the intervention, the greater the opportunity for resilience to manifest itself. Even so, some children, seemingly against all odds, rise above their circumstances.

References

Bandura, A. (1982) 'The psychology of chance encounters and life paths.' *American Psychologist 37*, 747–755.

Barnett, A. (1996) *Lives in the Balance: Age 27 Benefit-Cost Analysis of the High/Scope Perry Preschool Program.* Monographs of the High/Scope Educational Research Foundation No. 11. Ypsilanti, MI: The High/Scope Press.

Baumeister, A. and Kupstas, F. (1990) 'The new morbidity: Implications for prevention and amelioration.' In P.L.C. Evans and A.D.B. Clarke (eds) *Combating Mental Handicap.* Bicester: A.B. Academic.

Bell, R.Q. (1968) 'A reinterpretation of effects in studies of socialization.' *Psychological Review 75*, 81–95.

Belsky, J., Campbell, S.B., Cohn, J.F. and Moore, G. (1996) 'Instability of infant–parent attachment security.' *Developmental Psychology 32*, 921–924.

Benoit, D. and Parker, K.C.H. (1994) 'Stability and transmission of attachment across three generations.' *Child Development 65*, 1444–1456.

Berrueta-Clement, J.R., Schweinhart, L.J., Barnett, W.S., Epstein, A.S. and Weikart, D.D. (1984) *Changed Lives: The Effects of the Perry pre-school Program on Youths through Age 19.* Monographs of the High/Scope Educational Research Foundation. Ypsilanti, MI: High/Scope Press.

Binet, A. (1920) *Les Idées Modernes sur les Enfants.* Paris: Bibliothèque de Philosophie Scientifique.

Bisson, D. and De Schonen, E. (1994) *The Boy behind the Door.* London: Mandarin Paperbacks.

Blair, C. and Ramey, C.T. (1997) 'Early intervention for low-birth-weight infants and the path to second generation research.' In M.J. Guralnick (ed) *The Effectiveness of Early Intervention.* London: Paul H. Brookes.

Block, J. (1971) *Lives Through Time.* Berkeley, CA: Bancroft Books.

Block, J. (1980) 'From infancy to adulthood: A clarification.' *Child Development 51*, 622–623.

Bloom, B.S. (1964) *Stability and Change in Human Characteristics.* London: Wiley.

Bornstein, M.H. and Sigman, M.D. (1986) 'Continuity in mental development from infancy.' *Child Development 57*, 251–274.

Bowlby, J. (1946) *Forty-Four Juvenile Thieves: Their Characteristics and Home Life.* London: Ballière, Tindall and Cox.

Bowlby, J. (1951) *Maternal Care and Mental Health.* Geneva: World Health Organisation.

Bowlby, J. (1988) 'Developmental psychiatry comes of age.' *American Journal of Psychiatry 145,* 1–10.

Bowlby, J., Ainsworth, M.D., Boston, M. and Rosenbluth, D. (1956) 'The effects of mother–child separation: A follow-up study.' *British Journal of Medical Psychology 29,* 211–247.

Brim, O. and Kagan, J. (eds) (1980) *Constancy and Change in Human Development.* Cambridge, MA: Harvard Educational Press.

Bronfenbrenner, U. (1977) 'Toward an experimental ecology of human development.' *American Psychologist 32,* 513–531.

Bronfenbrenner, U. and Crouter, A.C. (1983) 'The evolution of environmental models in developmental research.' In P.H. Mussen (ed) *Handbook of Child Psychology,* Vol. 1. Chichester: John Wiley.

Brown, M. and Madge, N. (1982) *Despite the Welfare State.* London: Heinemann.

Brown, R.I. (1972) 'Cognitive changes in the adolescent slow learner.' *Journal of Child Psychology and Psychiatry 13,* 183–193.

Byng-Hall, J. (1997) 'The secure family base: Some implications for family therapy.' In G. Forrest (ed) *Bonding and Attachment: Current Issues in Research and Practice.* Occasional Paper No. 14. London: Association for Child Psychology and Psychiatry.

Campbell, F.A. and Ramey, C.T. (1999) Press conference handout on an age 21 follow-up of the Abecedarian Project, October 20th. Washington, DC: Department of Education.

Carlson, E.A.A. and Sroufe, L.A. (1995) 'Contributions of attachment theory to developmental psychopathology.' In D. Ciccheti and D.J. Cohen (eds) *Developmental Psychopathology,* Vol. 1. New York: Wiley.

Caspi, A., Elder, G.H. and Bem, D.J. (1988) 'Moving away from the world: Life course patterns of shy children.' *Developmental Quarterly 24,* 824–831.

Charles, D.C. (1953) 'Ability and accomplishment of persons earlier judged mentally deficient.' *Genetic Psychology Monographs 47,* 3–71.

Chess, S. and Thomas, A. (1984) *Origins and Evolution of Behavior Disorders.* New York: Brunner/Mazel.

Chess, S. and Thomas, A. (1999) *Goodness of Fit: Clinical Applications from Infancy through Adult Life.* Philadelphia: Brunner/Mazel.

Chisholm, K. (1998) 'A three-year follow-up of attachment and indiscriminate friendliness in children adopted from Romanian orphanages.' *Child Development 69*, 1092–1106.

Chisholm, K., Carter, M.C., Ames, E.W. and Morison, S.J. (1995) 'Attachment security and indiscriminately friendly behaviour in children adopted from Romanian orphanages.' *Development and Psychopathology 7*, 283–294.

Clarke, A.D.B. (1968) 'Learning and human development – the 42nd Maudsley Lecture.' *British Journal of Psychiatry 114*, 1061–1077.

Clarke, A.D.B. (1978) 'Presidential Address: Predicting human development: Problems, evidence, implications.' *Bulletin of the British Psychological Society 31*, 244–258.

Clarke, A.D.B. and Clarke, A.M. (1953) 'How constant is the IQ?' *Lancet ii*, 877–880.

Clarke, A.D.B. and Clarke, A.M. (1954) 'Cognitive changes in the feebleminded.' *British Journal of Psychology 45*, 173–179.

Clarke, A.D.B. and Clarke, A.M. (1959) 'Recovery from the effects of deprivation.' *Acta Psychologica 16*, 137–144.

Clarke, A.D.B. and Clarke, A.M. (1960) 'Recent advances in the study of deprivation.' *Journal of Child Psychology and Psychiatry 1*, 26–36.

Clarke, A.D.B. and Clarke, A.M. (1972) 'Consistency and variability in the growth of human characteristics.' In W.D. Wall and V.P. Varma (eds) *Advances in Educational Psychology*. London: University of London Press.

Clarke, A.D.B. and Clarke, A.M. (1981) 'Sleeper effects in development: Fact or artefact?' *Developmental Review 1*, 344–360.

Clarke, A.D.B. and Clarke, A.M. (1984) 'Constancy and change in growth of human characteristics.' *Journal of Child Psychology and Psychiatry 25*, 191–210.

Clarke, A.D.B. and Clarke, A.M. (1996) 'Varied destinies: A study of unfulfilled predictions.' In B. Bernstein and J. Brannen (eds) *Children, Research and Policy*. London: Taylor and Francis.

Clarke, A.D.B., Clarke, A.M. and Reiman, S. (1958) 'Cognitive and social changes in the feebleminded.' *British Journal of Psychology 49*, 144–157.

Clarke, A.M. (1982) 'Developmental discontinuities: An approach to assessing their nature.' In L.A. Bond and J.M. Joffe (eds) *Facilitating Infant and Early Childhood Development*. 58–79. Hanover, NH: University Press of New England.

Clarke, A.M. and Clarke, A.D.B. (eds) (1976) *Early Experience: Myth and Evidence*. London: Open Books. New York: Free Press.

Clarke, A.M. and Clarke A.D.B. (1982) 'Intervention and sleeper effects: A reply to Victoria Seitz.' *Developmental Review 2*, 76–86.

Clarke, A.M. and Clarke, A.D.B. (1988) 'The adult outcome of early behavioural abnormalities.' *International Journal of Behavioural Development 11*, 3–19.

Clarke, A. M. and Clarke, A.D.B. (1989) 'The later cognitive effects of early intervention – editorial.' *Intelligence 13*, 289–297.

Clarke, A.M. and Clarke, A.D.B. (1992) 'How modifiable is the human life path?' *International Review of Research in Mental Retardation 18*, 137–157.

Clarke, A.M., Clarke, A.D.B. and Berg, J.M. (eds) (1985) *Mental Deficiency: The Changing Outlook*, 4th edition. London: Methuen. New York: Free Press.

Curtiss, S. (1977) *Genie: A Psycholinguistic Study of a Modern-Day 'Wild Child'.* London: Academic Press.

Davis, K. (1940) 'Extreme social isolation of a child.' *American Journal of Sociology 45*, 554–565.

Davis, K. (1947) 'Final note on a case of extreme isolation.' *American Journal of Sociology 52*, 432–437.

Dearborn, W.F. and Rothney, J.M.W. (1941) *Predicting the Child's Development.* Cambridge, Mass.: Sci-Art Publishers.

Douglas, J.W.B. (1975) 'Early hospital admissions and later disturbances of behaviour and learning.' *Developmental Medicine and Child Neurology 17*, 456–480.

Dumaret, A-C., Coppel-Batsch, M. and Couraud, S. (1997) 'Adult outcome of children reared for long-term periods in foster families.' *Child Abuse and Neglect 21*, 911–927.

Duyme, M., Dumaret, A-L. and Tomkiewicz, S. (1999) 'How can we boost IQs of "dull children"?: A late adoption study.' *Proceedings of the National Academy of Science 96*, 8790–94.

Elder, G.H. (1974) *Children of the Great Depression: Social Change in Life Experience.* Chicago: University of Chicago Press.

Elder, G.H. (1998) 'The life course as developmental theory.' *Child Development 69*, 1–12.

Essen, J. and Wedge, P. (1982) *Continuities in Childhood Disadvantage.* London: Heinemann.

Esser, G., Schmidt, M.H. and Woerner, W. (1990) 'Epidemiology and course of psychiatric disorder in school aged children – results of a longitudinal study.' *Journal of Child Psychology and Psychiatry 31*, 243–263.

Ferguson, D.M., Horwood, L.J. and Lynskey, M. (1994) 'The childhoods of multiple problem adolescents: A 15-year longitudinal study.' *Journal of Child Psychology and Psychiatry 35*, 1123–1140.

Fonagy, P., Steele, H. and Steele, M. (1991) 'Maternal representations of attachment predict the organization of infant–mother attachment at one year of age.' *Child Development 62*, 891–905.

Fonagy, P., Steele, M., Steele, H., Higgitt, A. and Target, M. (1994) 'The Emanuel Miller Memorial Lecture, 1992. The theory and practice of resilience.' *Journal of Child Psychology and Psychiatry 35*, 231–257.

Fox, N.A., Kimmerley, N.L. and Schafer, W.D. (1991) 'Attachment to mother/attachment to father: A meta-analysis.' *Child Development 62*, 210–225.

Freud, A. and Dann, S. (1951) 'An experiment in group upbringing.' *Psycho-Analytic Study of the Child 6*, 127–165.

Freud, S. (1910) 'Infantile sexuality. Three contributions to the Sexual theory.' Translated by A.A. Brill. *Nervous and Mental Disease Monographs* No. 7.

Freud, S. (1949) *An Outline of Psycho-Analysis.* London: Hogarth Press.

Garber, H.L. (1988) *The Milwaukee Project: Preventing Mental Retardation in Children at Risk.* Washington, DC: American Association on Mental Retardation.

Goldfarb, W. (1943) 'The effects of early institutional care on adolescent personality.' *Journal of Experimental Education 12*, 106–129.

Goldsmith, H.H. and Alansky, J.A. (1987) 'Maternal and infant temperamental predictors of attachment: A meta-analytic review.' *Journal of Consulting and Clinical Psychology 55*, 805–816.

Greenough, W.T., Black, J.E. and Wallace, C.S. (1987) 'Experience and brain development.' *Child Development 58*, 539–559.

Guralnick, M.J. (1997) 'Second-generation research in the field of early intervention.' In M.J. Guralnick (ed) *The Effectiveness of Early Intervention.* London: Paul H. Brookes.

Haggerty, R.J., Roughman, K.J. and Pless, I.V. (1975) *Child Health and Community.* New York: Wiley.

Harlow, H.F. (1963) 'The maternal affectional system.' In B.M. Foss (ed) *Determinants of Infant Behaviour.* London: Methuen.

Heber, R.F., Dever, R.B. and Conry, R.J. (1968) 'The influence of environmental and genetic variables on intellectual development.' In H.J. Prehm, L.J. Hamerlynck and J.E. Crosson (eds) *Behavioral Research in Mental Retardation.* Eugene: University of Oregon Press.

Hilton, M.R. and Mezey, G.C. (1996) 'Victims and perpetrators of child sexual abuse.' *British Journal of Psychiatry 169*, 408–415.

Hindley, C.B. and Owen, C.F. (1978) 'The extent of individual changes in IQ for ages between 6 months and 17 years in a British longitudinal sample.' *Journal of Child Psychology and Psychiatry 19*, 329–350.

Hodges, J. and Tizard, B. (1989) 'Social and family relationships of ex-institutional adolescents.' *Journal of Child Psychology and Psychiatry 30*, 77–98.

Holmes, J. (1993) 'Attachment theory: A biological basis for psychotherapy?' *British Journal of Psychiatry 163*, 430–438.

Holmes, J. (1998) 'Psychodynamics, narrative and intentional causality.' *British Journal of Psychiatry 173*, 279–280.

Home Office (1999) *Sex Offending against Children: Understanding the Risk.* London: Home Office.

The Independent (1999) 'Councils named in adoption crisis', 7 April.

Infant Health and Development Program (IHDP) (1990) 'Enhancing the outcomes of low-birth-weight, premature infants.' *Journal of the American Medical Association 263*, 3035–3042.

Kadushin, A. (1970) *Adopting Older Children.* New York: Columbia University Press.

Kagan, J. (1979) *The Growth of the Child.* London: Methuen.

Kagan, J. (1992) 'Yesterday's premises, tomorrow's promises.' *Developmental Psychology 28*, 990–997.

Kagan, J. (1997) 'Temperament and reactions to unfamiliarity.' *Child Development 68*, 139–143.

Kagan, J. (1998) *Three Seductive Ideas.* Cambridge, Mass. and London: Harvard University Press.

Kagan, J. and Moss, H.A. (1962) *Birth to Maturity.* New York: Wiley.

Kagan, J. and Snidman, N. (1991) 'Temperamental factors in human development.' *American Psychologist 46*, 856–862.

Kerr, M., Lambert, W.W. and Bem, D.J. (1996) 'Life course sequelae of childhood shyness in Sweden: Comparison with the United States.' *Developmental Psychology 32*, 1100–1105.

Kerr, M., Lambert, W.W., Stattin, H. and Klackenberg-Larsen, I. (1994) 'Stability of inhibition in a Swedish longitudinal sample.' *Child Development 65*, 138–146.

Kirk, S.A. (1958) *Early Education of the Mentally Retarded.* Urbana, Ill.: University of Illinois Press.

Kohnstamm, D. and Mervielde, I. (1998) 'Personality development.' In A. Demetriou, W. Doise and C. van Lieshout (eds) *Life-Span Developmental Psychology*. Chichester: John Wiley.

Koluchová, J. (1972) 'Severe deprivation in twins: A case study.' *Journal of Child Psychology and Psychiatry 13*, 107–114.

Koluchová, J. (1976) 'A report on the further development of twins after severe and prolonged deprivation.' In A.M. Clarke and A.D.B. Clarke (eds) *Early Experience: Myth and Evidence*. London: Open Books. New York: Free Press.

Koluchová, J. (1991) 'Severely deprived twins after 22 years' observation.' *Studia Psychologica 33*, 23–28.

Kolvin, I., Miller, F.J.W., Scott, D. McI., Gatzanis, S.R.M. and Fleeting, M. (1990) *Continuities of Deprivation? The Newcastle 1000 Family Study*. Aldershot: Gower House.

Laucht, M., Esser, G. and Schmidt, M. (1994) 'Contrasting infant predictors of later cognitive functioning.' *Journal of Child Psychology and Psychiatry 35*, 649–662.

Lazar, I. and Darlington, R.B. (1978) *Lasting Effects after pre-school*. Washington, DC: DHEW Publication No. (OHDS) 79-30178.

Lazar, I. and Darlington, R.B. (1982) 'Lasting effects of early education.' *Monographs of the Society for Research in Child Development 47*, 1–51.

Lazar, I., Hubbell, V.R., Murray, H., Rosche, M. and Royce, J. (1977) *The Persistence of pre-school Effects: A Long-Term Follow-Up of Fourteen Experiments*. Washington, DC: The Consortium on Developmental Continuity, Education Commission of the States. DHEW Publication No. (OHDS) 78-30130.

Lenneberg, E.H. (1967) *Biological Foundations of Language*. New York: Wiley.

Levine, S. (1960) 'Stimulation in infancy.' *Scientific American 202*, 80–86.

Lewis, H. (1954) *Deprived Children*. London: Oxford University Press.

MacFarlane, J.W. (1964) 'Perspectives on personality consistency and change from the Guidance Study.' *Vita Humana 7*, 115–126.

Magnusson, D. (1991) 'Individual development in a longitudinal perspective.' *Reports from the Department of Psychology, Stockholm University*, No. 773.

Malson, L. (1972) *Wolf Children*. London: NLB.

Mason, M.K. (1942) 'Learning to speak after six and a half years of silence.' *Journal of Speech Disorders 7*, 295–304.

McCall, R.E. and Carriger, M.S. (1993) 'A meta-analysis of infant habituation and recognition performance as predictors of later IQ.' *Child Development 64*, 57–79.

Mednick, S.A. and Baert, A.E. (eds) (1981) *Prospective Longitudinal Research: An Empirical Basis for the Primary Prevention of Psychosocial Disorders.* Oxford: Oxford University Press on behalf of the WHO Regional Office for Europe.

Melhuish, E. (1993) 'A measure of love? An overview of the assessment of attachment.' *ACPP Review and Newsletter 15,* 269–275.

Milosz, C. (1988) *Native Realm: A Search for Self Definition.* Harmondsworth: Penguin Books.

Minty, B. (1999) Annotation: Outcomes in long-term foster family care. *Journal of Child Psychology and Psychiatry 40,* 991–999.

Moffitt, T.E., Caspi, A., Harkness, H.R. and Silva, P.A. (1993) 'The natural history of change in intellectual performance: Who changes? How much? Is it meaningful?' *Journal of Child Psychology and Psychiatry 34,* 455–506.

Morgan, P. (1998) *Adoption and the Care of Children: The British and American Experience.* London: Institute of Economic Affairs Health and Welfare Unit.

Moskowitz, S. (1985) 'Longitudinal follow-up of child survivors of the Holocaust.' *American Academy of Child Psychiatry 24,* 401–407.

Mullen, P.E., Martin, J.L., Anderson, J.C., Romans, S.E. and Herbison, G.P. (1993) 'Childhood sexual abuse and mental health in adult life.' *British Journal of Psychiatry 163,* 271–332.

Mullen, P.E., Martin, J.L., Anderson, J.C., Romans, S.E. and Herbison, G.P. (1994) 'The effect of child sexual abuse on social, interpersonal and sexual function in adult life.' *British Journal of Psychiatry 165,* 35–47.

Nemzek, C.L. (1933) 'The constancy of the IQ.' *Psychological Bulletin 30,* 143–168.

Novak, M.A. and Harlow, H.F. (1975) 'Social recovery of monkeys isolated for the first year of life: I. Rehabilitation and therapy.' *Developmental Psychology 11,* 453–465.

O'Connor, T.G. and the English and Romanian Adoptees Study Team (1999a) 'The effects of global severe privation on cognitive competence.' *Child Development, in press.*

O'Connor, T.G., Thorpe, K., Dunn, J. and Golding, J. (1999b) 'Parental divorce and adjustment in adulthood: Findings from a community sample.' *Journal of Child Psychology and Psychiatry 40,* 777–789.

Oden, M.H. (1968) 'The fulfilment of promise: 40-year follow-up of the Terman Gifted Group.' *Genetic Psychology Monographs 77,* 3–93.

Orlansky, H. (1949) 'Infant care and personality.' *Psychological Review 46,* 1–48.

Pilling, D. (1990) *Escape from Disadvantage.* London: Falmer Press.

Plomin, R. (1994) 'Genetic research and identification of environmental influences: Emanuel Miller Memorial Lecture.' *Journal of Child Psychology and Psychiatry 35*, 817–834.

Plomin, R. and Dunn, J. (eds) (1986) *The Study of Temperament: Changes, Continuities and Challenges.* London: Lawrence Erlbaum.

Prugh, D.G., Staub, E.M., Sands, H.H., Kirschbaum, R.M. and Lenihan, E.A. (1953) 'A study of the emotional reactions of children and families to hospitalization and illness.' *American Journal of Orthopsychiatry 23*, 70–106.

Quinton, D. and Rutter, M. (1984a) 'Parents with children in care: I. Current circumstances and parenting.' *Journal of Child Psychology and Psychiatry 25*, 211–229.

Quinton, D. and Rutter, M. (1984b) 'Parents with children in care: II. Intergenerational continuities.' *Journal of Child Psychology and Psychiatry 25*, 231–250.

Quinton, D., Rutter, M., Dowdney, L., Liddle, C., Mrazek, D. and Skuse, D. (1982) *Childhood Experience and Parenting Behaviour.* Final Report to the Social Science Research Council, UK.

Ramey, C.T. (1982) Commentary on 'Lasting effects of early education: A report from the Consortium for Longitudinal Studies.' In I. Lazar and R. Darlington (eds) *Monographs of the Society for Research in Child Development 47*, 2–3.

Ramey, C.T. (1988) 'Educational intervention for high-risk children.' Abstract in program for *Key Issues in Mental Retardation Research.* 8th World Congress of the IASSMD, Dublin.

Ramey, C.T. and Campbell, F.A. (1981) 'Educational intervention for children at risk for mild retardation: A longitudinal analysis.' In P. Mittler (ed) *Frontiers of Knowledge in Mental Retardation (Vol. I): Social, Educational and Behavioral Aspects.* Baltimore, MD: University Park Press.

Ramey, C.T. and Campbell, F.A. (1987) 'The Carolina Abecedarian Project: An educational experiment concerning human malleability.' In J.J. Gallagher and C.T. Ramey (eds) *The Malleability of Children.* Baltimore, MD: Paul H. Brookes.

Ramey, C.T. and Haskins, R. (1981) 'The modification of intelligence through early experience.' *Intelligence 5*, 5–19.

Ramey, C.T. and Ramey, S. (1992) 'Effective early intervention.' *Mental Retardation 30*, 337–345.

Rathbun, C., DiVirgilio, L. and Waldfogel, S. (1958) 'The restitutive process in children following radical separation from family and culture.' *American Journal of Orthopsychiatry 28*, 403–415.

Rathbun, C., McLaughlin, H., Bennett, O. and Garland, J.A. (1965) 'Later adjustment of children following radical separation from family and culture.' *American Journal of Orthopsychiatry 35,* 604–609.

Richardson, S.A. (1985) 'Epidemiology.' In A.M. Clarke, A.D.B. Clarke and J.M. Berg (eds) *Mental Deficiency: The Changing Outlook,* 4th edition. London: Methuen. New York: Free Press.

Rodgers, B. (1990) 'Behaviour and personality in childhood as predictors of adult psychiatric disorder.' *Journal of Child Psychology and Psychiatry 31,* 393–414.

Roswell Harris, D. (1958) 'Some aspects of cognitive and personality test changes in a group of 100 feebleminded young men.' Unpublished MA thesis, University of Reading.

Royce, J.M., Lazar, I. and Darlington, R.B. (1983) 'Minority families, early education and later life chances.' *American Journal of Orthopsychiatry 53,* 706–720.

Rutter, M. (1989) 'Pathways from childhood to adult life.' *Journal of Child Psychology and Psychiatry 30,* 23–51.

Rutter, M. (1995) 'Clinical implications of attachment concepts.' *Journal of Child Psychology and Psychiatry 36,* 549–571.

Rutter, M. (1999) 'Psychosocial adversity and child psychopathology.' *British Journal of Psychiatry 174,* 480–493.

Rutter, M., Cox, A., Tupling, C., Berger, M. and Yule, W. (1975a) 'Attainment and adjustment in two geographical areas: I. The prevalence of psychiatric disorder.' *British Journal of Psychiatry 126,* 493–509.

Rutter, M., Yule, B., Quinton, D., Rowlands, O., Yule, W. and Berger, M. (1975b) 'Attainment and adjustment in two geographical areas: III. Some factors accounting for area differences.' *British Journal of Psychiatry 126,* 520–533.

Rutter, M. and Madge, N. (1976) *Cycles of Disadvantage.* London: Heinemann.

Rutter, M., Quinton, D. and Liddle, C. (1983) 'Parenting in two generations: Looking backwards and looking forwards.' In N. Madge (ed) *Families at Risk.* London: Heinemann.

Rutter, M. and Sandberg, S. (1985) 'Epidemiology of child psychiatric disorder: Methodological issues and some substantive findings.' *Child Psychiatry and Human Development 15,* 209–233.

Rutter, M. and the English and Romanian Adoptees (ERA) Study Team (1998) 'Developmental catch-up, and deficit, following and after severe global early privation.' *Journal of Child Psychology and Psychiatry 39,* 465–476.

Rutter, M., Silberg, J., O'Connor, T. and Simonoff, E. (1999a) 'Genetics and child psychiatry: I. Advances in quantitative and molecular genetics.' *Journal of Child Psychology and Psychiatry 40*, 3–18.

Rutter, M., Anderson-Wood, L., Beckett, C., Bredenkamp, D., Castle, J., Groothues, C., Kreppner, K., Keaveney, L., Lord, C., O'Connor, T.G. and the ERA Study Team (1999b) 'Quasi-autistic patterns following severe early privation.' *Journal of Child Psychology and Psychiatry 40*, 537–549.

Sadowski, H., Ugarte, B., Kolvin, I., Kaplan, C. and Barnes, J. (1999) 'Early life disadvantages and major depression in adulthood.' *British Journal of Psychiatry 174*, 112–120.

Sameroff, A.J. and Chandler, M.J. (1975) 'Reproductive risk and the continuum of caretaking causality.' In F.D. Horowitz, M. Hetherington, S. Scarr-Salapatek and G. Siegel (eds) *Review of Child Development Research*, Vol. 4. Chicago: University of Chicago Press.

Scarr, S. and McCartney, K. (1983) 'How people make their own environments: A theory of genotype-environment effects.' *Child Development 54*, 424–435.

Schaffer, H.R. (1958) 'Objective observations of personality development in early infancy.' *British Journal of Medical Psychology 31*, 174–183.

Schaffer, H.R. (1992) 'Early experience and the parent–child relationship: Genetic and environmental interactions as developmental determinants.' In B. Tizard and V. Varma (eds) *Vulnerability and Resilience in Human Development*. London: Jessica Kingsley Publishers.

Schaffer, H.R. (2000) 'The early experience assumption: Past, present and future.' *International Journal of Behavioural Development, in press*.

Scheerens, J. (1987) *Enhancing Educational Opportunities for Disadvantaged Learners: A Review of Dutch Research on Compensatory Education and Educational Development Policy*. Oxford: North Holland Publishing Company.

Schweinhart, L.J. and Weikart, D.P. (1980) *Young Children Grow Up: The Effects of the Perry pre-school Program on Youth through Age 15. Monographs of the High/Scope Educational Research Foundation*. Ypsilanti, MI: High/Scope Press.

Schweinhart, L.J. and Weikart, D.P. (1981) 'Perry pre-school effects nine years later. What do they mean?' In M.J. Begab, H.C. Haywood and H. Garber (eds) *Psychosocial Influences on Retarded Development*, Vol. 2. Baltimore, MD: University Park Press.

Scott, J.P. (1963) 'The process of primary socialization in canine and human infants.' *Monographs of the Society for Research in Child Development 28*, 1–47.

Scott, J.P. (1968) *Early Experience and the Organization of Behavior*. Belmont, CA: Brooks/Cole.

Skeels, H.M. (1966) 'Adult status of children with contrasting early life histories.' *Monographs of the Society for Research in Child Development 31*, 3, 1–65.

Skeels, H.M. and Dye, H.B. (1939) 'A study of the effects of differential stimulation on mentally retarded children.' *Proceedings of the American Association on Mental Deficiency 44*, 114–136.

Skuse, D. (1984) 'Extreme deprivation in early childhood: II. Theoretical issues and a comparative review.' *Journal of Child Psychology and Psychiatry 25*, 543–572.

Skuse, D., Pickles, A., Wolke, D. and Reilly, S. (1994) 'Postnatal growth and mental development: Evidence for a "sensitive" period.' *Journal of Child Psychology and Psychiatry 35*, 521–545.

Slater, A. (1995) 'Individual differences in infancy and later IQ.' *Journal of Child Psychology and Psychiatry 36*, 69–112.

Slater, A., Cooper, R., Rose, D. and Morison, V. (1989) 'Predicting cognitive performance from infancy to early childhood.' *Human Development 32*, 158–166.

Spearman, C. (1904) 'General intelligence: Objectively determined and measured.' *American Journal of Psychology 115*, 201–292.

Spitz, R.A. (1945) 'Hospitalism: An enquiry into the genesis of psychiatric conditions in early childhood.' *Psycho-Analytic Study of the Child 1*, 53–74.

Spitz, R.A. (1946a) 'Hospitalism: A follow-up report on an investigation described in Volume I, 1945.' *Psycho-Analytic Study of the Child 2*, 113–117.

Spitz, R.A. (1946b) 'Anaclitic depression: II. An inquiry into the genesis of psychiatric conditions in early childhood.' *Psycho-Analytic Study of the Child 2*, 313–342.

Sroufe, L.A., Egeland, B. and Kreuzer, T. (1990) 'The fate of early experience following developmental change: Longitudinal approaches to individual adaptation in childhood.' *Child Development 61*, 1363–1373.

Steele, H., Steele, M. and Fonagy, P. (1995) 'Associations among attachment classifications of mothers, fathers and infants.' *Child Development 67*, 541–555.

Stevenson, I. (1957) 'Is the human personality more plastic in infancy and childhood?' *American Journal of Psychiatry 114*, 152–161.

Stevenson, J. (1999) 'The treatment of the long-term *sequelae* of child abuse.' *Journal of Child Psychology and Psychiatry 40*, 89–111.

Suomi, S.J. and Harlow, H.F. (1972) Social rehabilitation of isolate-reared monkeys. *Developmental Psychology 6*, 487–496.

Svendsen, D. (1982) Changes in IQ: Environmental and individual factors. A follow up study of former slow learners. *Journal of Child Psychology and Psychiatry 23*, 69–74.

Svendsen, D. (1983) Factors related to changes in IQ: A follow up study of former slow learners. *Journal of Child Psychology and Psychiatry 24*, 405–413.

Thomas, A. and Chess, S. (1976) 'Evolution of behavior disorders into adolescence.' *American Journal of Psychiatry 133*, 539–542.

Thomas, A. and Chess, S. (1977) *Temperament and Development.* New York: Brunner/Mazel.

Thomas, A. and Chess, S. (1980) *The Dynamics of Psychological Development.* New York: Brunner/Mazel.

Thomas, A., Chess, S. and Birch, H.G. (1968) *Temperament and Behaviour Disorders.* New York: New York University Press.

Thompson, A. (1986) 'Adam – a severely deprived Colombian orphan.' *Journal of Child Psychology and Psychiatry 27*, 689–695.

Thorndike, R.L. (1933) 'The effect of the interval between test and retest on the constancy of the IQ.' *Journal of Educational Psychology 24*, 543–549.

Thorndike, R.L. (1940) '"Constancy" of the IQ.' *Psychological Bulletin 37*, 167–186.

Tizard, B. (1977) *Adoption: A Second Chance.* London: Open Books.

Tonge, W.L., Lunn, J.E., Greathead, M., McLaren, S. and Bosanko, C. (1983) 'Generations of problem families in Sheffield.' In N. Madge (ed) *Families At Risk.* London: Heinemann.

Triseliotis, J. and Russell, J. (1984) *Hard to Place: The Outcome of Adoption and Residential Care.* London: Heinemann.

US Department of Health and Human Services (1985) *The Impact of Head Start on Children, Families and Communities: Head Start Synthesis Project.* Washington, DC: CSR, Incorporated Contract No. 105-81-C-026.

Von Knorring, A-L., Andersson, O. and Magnusson, D. (1987) 'Psychiatric care and course of psychiatric disorders from childhood to early adulthood in a representative sample.' *Journal of Child Psychology and Psychiatry 28*, 324–341.

Wachs, T.D. and Gruen, G.E. (1982) *Early Experience and Human Development.* New York: Plenum Press.

Waddington, C.H. (1966) *Principles of Development and Differentiation.* New York: Macmillan.

Waterhouse, L., Dobash, R.P. and Carnie, J. (1994) *Child Sexual Abuse.* Edinburgh: The Scottish Office Central Research Unit.

Watson, J.B. (1928) *Psychological Care of Infant and Child.* New York: Norton.

Wedge, P. and Prosser, H. (1973) *Born to Fail?* London: Arrow Books.

Werner, E.E. (1985) 'Stress and protective factors in children's lives.' In A.R. Nicol (ed) *Studies in Child Psychology and Psychiatry.* London: Wiley.

Werner, E.E. (1989) 'High-risk children in young adulthood: A longitudinal study from birth to 32 years.' *American Journal of Orthopsychiatry 59,* 72–81.

Werner, E.E. and Smith, R.S. (1982) *Vulnerable but Invincible: A Longitudinal Study of Resilient Children and Youth.* New York: McGraw-Hill.

Wilson, R.S. (1985) 'The Louisville Twin Study: Developmental synchronies in behavior.' *Child Development 54,* 298–316.

Wolke, D., Söhne, B., Ohrt, B. and Riegel, K. (1995) 'Follow-up of preterm children: Important to document dropouts.' *Lancet 345,* 447.

Wolkind, S., Kruk, S. and Chaves, L. (1976) 'Childhood separation experiences and psycho-social status in primiparous women: Preliminary findings.' *British Journal of Psychiatry 128,* 391–396.

Yule, W., Gold, D.R. and Busch, C. (1982) 'Long-term predictive validity of the WPPSI: An 11-year follow-up study.' *Personality and Individual Differences 3,* 65–71.

Zigler, E. and Valentine, J. (eds) (1979) *Project Head Start: A Legacy of the War on Poverty.* New York: Free Press.

Subject Index

Author Index